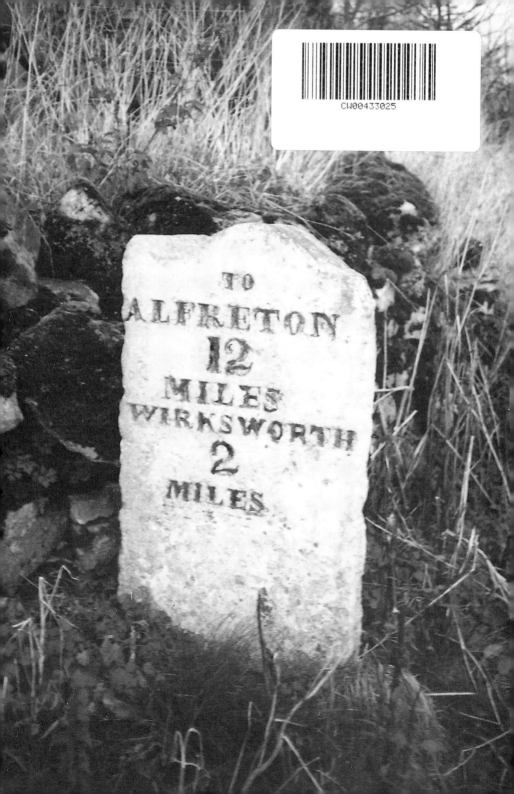

Previous page: a milestone produced by a local stone-mason long before motor cars appeared on the roads of Derbyshire.

Walking from your car
in
Derbyshire

Astrid & Ray Russell

Copyright © Astrid and Ray Russell, 1995

All Rights Reserved. No part of this publication may be reproduced, stored in a retrieval system, or transmitted in any form or by any means – electronic, mechanical, photocopying, recording, or otherwise – without prior written permission from the publisher.

Published by Sigma Leisure – an imprint of
Sigma Press, 1 South Oak Lane, Wilmslow, Cheshire SK9 6AR, England.

British Library Cataloguing in Publication Data
A CIP record for this book is available from the British Library.

ISBN: 1-85058-437-0

Typesetting and Design by: Sigma Press, Wilmslow, Cheshire.

Cover photograph: The Upper Dove Valley, near Crowdecote

Maps and photographs: the authors

Illustrations: Helena Russell

Printed by: Manchester Free Press

Contents

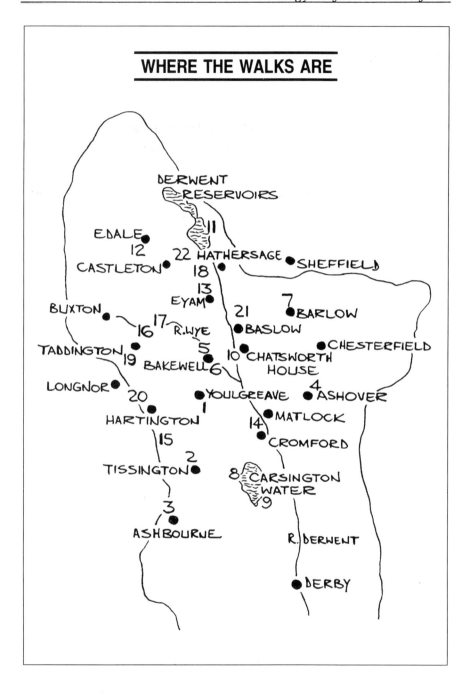

Introduction

The Derbyshire Peak District is, understandably, a much visited part of Britain. Its contrasting scenery, from high, heathery moorland to deep, wooded limestone dales, attracted many people even before the creation of the Peak National Park. The history of the region, from prehistoric times to the early industrial age, is still much in evidence and provides interest in all sorts of ways. Routes established by the area's inhabitants in travelling between their farms, churches, mines and markets over many centuries, remain as a network of footpaths and lanes, offering much enjoyment to today's walkers.

This is a collection of 22 moderate walks – all of them circular and none too strenuous. They offer ample opportunity to explore and enjoy the very varied landscape and history of Derbyshire. Whilst many of the county's famous beauty spots and interesting features are visited, some less-frequented paths are also followed. The outstanding views over both limestone and gritstone – the White and the Dark Peaks – form an important element of the walks.

The routes are mostly in the Derbyshire Peak District, but some have been included in the lesser-known but equally attractive areas on the southern and eastern edges of the Peak National Park.

The walks are mainly in the six to eight mile range and each could be either a half-day's brisk exercise or a full day's more leisurely ramble. Many include a pub or other possible refreshment stop along the way. Most country walks can have wet or muddy points at any time of the year so unless the weather is exceptionally dry we would advise that wellies or walking boots are always worn. If walking with children, be alert to the possible hazards which exist in the countryside – rivers, old industrial workings, steep banks and mine shafts can be dangerous places!

We have tried to ensure that the walk descriptions are accurate but changes, such as the erection of a temporary fence or the replacement or realigning of a stile or a gate, can occur. All routes have been recently walked and should therefore be followed without difficulty. However, if you come across an obstruction to the right of way you are following do bring it to the attention of the local council. It has the right by law to take responsibility for clearing the obstruction if, as occasionally happens, the landowner cannot be persuaded to do it.

The walks in this book give us continuing pleasure – we hope they give you similar enjoyment. Every care has been taken to ensure that the information given in this book is reliable. However, the authors accept no responsibility for inaccuracy.

Maps

It is intended that all walks can be followed from the descriptions given. However, use of the appropriate Ordnance Survey map will provide additional information and help clarify routes if uncertainty occasionally arises. Ordnance Survey maps particularly useful with this book are: 'The Dark Peak' and 'The White Peak' (both Outdoor Leisure Series).

The Country Code:

Enjoy the countryside and respect its life and work

Guard against all risk of fire

Fasten all gates

Keep your dogs under close control

Keep to public paths across farmland

Use gates and stiles to cross fences, hedges and walls

Leave livestock, crops and machinery alone

Take your litter home

Help to keep all water clean

Protect wildlife, plants and trees

Take special care on country roads

Make no unnecessary noise

Unfamiliar Words and Phrases

The following words and phrases arise in the walk descriptions and may be unfamiliar:

Clapper bridge   A simple bridge made from flat stone slabs placed across upright stone pillars.

Enclosures   Fields formed by putting walls or hedges around an area of common land.

Folly	A costly structure with little purpose other than to satisfy a whim of its owner. These were popular with wealthy Victorians and often took the form of a tower or castle.
Holloway	Before roads were surfaced, heavily used routes often became worn down below the level of the surrounding land, thus becoming hollowed.
Hydro	An establishment offering a variety of water cures or "hydrotherapy" usually based on a local spring's reputed healing qualities.
Jagger	The person in charge of a string of packhorses.
Motte and Bailey	A defensive construction made up of an earth mound surrounded by a ditch.
Pinfold	A small enclosure in a village where stray animals were penned until their owners paid a fine for their release.
Ridge and Furrow	Parallel ridges sometimes seen on pasture land showing where in mediaeval times the land was ploughed and cultivated in long strips for individual villagers.
Turnpikes	From the mid-18th century Acts of Parliament were passed allowing Trusts to collect tolls from users of a particular stretch of highway in order to pay for improvements to the roads. Such roads were known as turnpikes.

Walk 1:
Alport, Harthill Moor and Bradford Dale

Footpaths and quiet roads give varying views of the village of Youlgreave and its setting. The final stretch is along the delightful Bradford Dale.

Fairly easy walking with several gradual climbs.

Distance: *6 miles (10km).*

Parking: *Above the bridge over the River Lathkill at Alport. Map reference 220646.*

Walk down the road, cross the River Lathkill and turn right down a narrow road between cottages to a bridge just above a disused mill. This is an idyllic spot now but it was not always so. Below the mill was a thriving lead smelting site with all its attendant noise and deadly fumes. Trees now cover the remains of the flues which carried the fumes up the steep hillside to a chimney at the top. Keep to this road as it turns right over the bridge and continue uphill around two sharp bends. Now follow this quiet, pleasant road for some distance, enjoying extensive views towards Stanton Moor on the left and Youlgreave on the right. Visible above the trees ahead are the twin pinnacles of Robin Hood's Stride, a rocky outcrop which was also known as Mock Beggars Hall because its outline looked like the towers of a mansion.

After climbing steeply through a wood look out for a wide

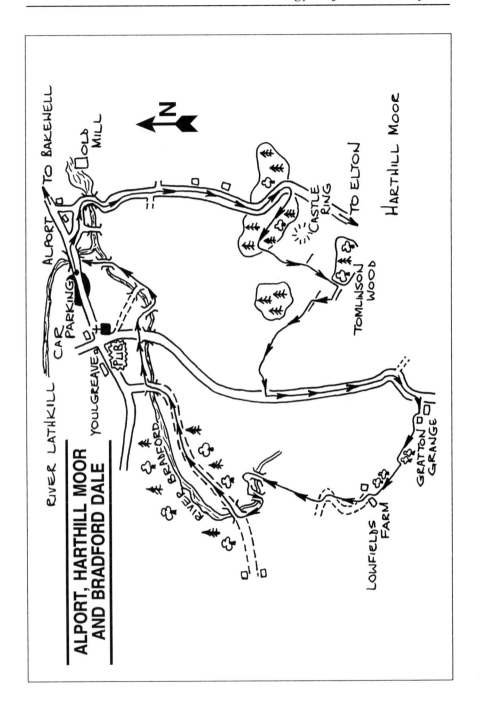

footpath leading into the trees on the right, where on the left-hand side of the road there are open fields again. The clear path becomes narrower and eventually crosses a stile at the end of the wood. Bear slightly right down a field to cross another stile over a semi-derelict wall and turn left to continue on a wide track. At the top of the hill on your left is Castle Ring, an Iron Age hill fort. Follow the track until it turns left, where you keep straight ahead in the direction of Elton. Go through a squeezer stile then bear right to climb the next field following the over-head cables to a gateway.

Don't go through the gateway but turn right, towards Youl-greave, and walk with the wall on your left for a short way to a footpath sign. Bear right in the direction indicated, to another footpath sign on the opposite side of the field. Looking back from this field you get a good view of Castle Ring – the ramparts and ditch are quite clearly defined. Go through a gap in the wall and walk beside the wall on your left, climbing a stile at the end of the field. Now bear slightly right up the next field, passing a walled enclosure, to reach another squeezer stile, then continue to a gateway. Keep straight ahead to the next stile on the right of a large tree. Cross the farm track beyond and go straight ahead over two fields keeping to the contour in the first, then climbing the second to a step stile over the wall at the top.

Follow the path down to a minor road and turn left into it. It soon levels out and passes a small quarry. There are fine open views from this stretch. Further on, the road bends sharply right and goes downhill. Leave the road at the first farm on the right – Gratton Grange – noticing the cart shed with its beautifully carved stone pillars and date of 1853. Bear right to pass behind the farmhouse and go through a metal gate into a field. Bear slightly right to another gate and then go straight ahead to a stile. Continue beside a fence on the left, then cross a stile on your left to continue – in the same direction as before – to

Lowfields Farm. Cross the farmyard and go through a gate on the right of the farmhouse. Now follow the farm drive down the hill to cross a cattle grid and a small brook at the bottom.

A few steps along a walled lane, cross a stile on your right and continue with a wall on your right. Pass a barn then go through a small enclosure. Climb a stile at the far side and go straight ahead over three more stiles. After passing beneath overhead cables bear slightly left to cross a footbridge over the infant River Bradford. Turn left and climb slightly on a clear path, go down some wooden steps and turn right to another footbridge. Cross the bridge and turn right to soon reach a wider track.

Turn right into this track and you will see evidence of the former activities carried on here. Upstream (to your right) a small dam provided power, via a head race, to a small bobbin mill on the opposite side of the track. The dam also supplied water to the sheep dipping area constructed between the track and the dam. Continue on this track beside the River Bradford through a delightful tree-lined dale. A little way along, on the opposite bank, are the ruins of a small flour mill, again powered by the river. Further along is a series of ponds which probably developed from fish ponds that in the Middle Ages supplied fresh fish. Many villages away from the sea had similar ponds. Now they provide a habitat for many water birds such as dippers, little grebes and wagtails.

The route eventually goes through a small gate and crosses a clapper bridge beside a ford. Go through a stile on the right and continue, now with the river on your right. On reaching a surfaced lane cross it and go straight ahead on a rough track which soon crosses the river and continues beside it, passing a fine packhorse bridge where an old lane descends from Youlgreave. Keep on until you finally regain the road at Alport.

Packhorse bridge over the River Bradford

Walk 2:
Alsop-en-le-Dale, Parwich
and Tissington

*Three delightful limestone villages are linked by quiet field
paths and a stretch of a former railway line – now the
Tissington Trail.*

A fairly easy walk with only gentle gradients.

Distance: *6 miles (10km).*

Parking: *Alsop-en-le-Dale station (on the Tissington Trail).
Map reference 156548.*

In 1967 the Ashbourne-Buxton branch of the LNWR finally
closed completely and the line was purchased by the Peak Park
and made into a 'trail' for walkers, cyclists and horse riders. The
Tissington Trail provides easy walking and some very fine
views of the surrounding countryside. The sites of the stations
are now car parks and the roads and footpaths which cross the
Trail provide access points.

From the car park walk a few steps to the left along the Trail
then turn right through a squeezer stile on a footpath signposted to Alsop-en-le-Dale. About halfway down the hill go
through a stile on your right and continue, with the wall now
on your left, to reach a minor road. Turn right and walk through
Alsop-en-le-Dale. The church has exceptionally thick walls and
several Norman features, including the south doorway. Oppo-

ALSOP-EN-LE-DALE, PARWICH AND TISSINGTON

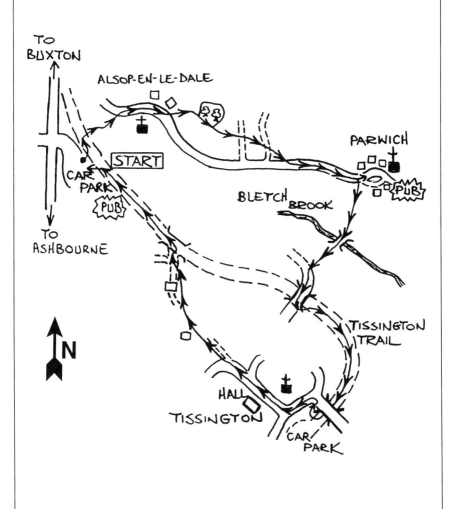

site the church is Alsop Hall, whose original owners gave the village its name.

Immediately beyond the last house on the left, turn left through a stile and cross the field to a stile by a footpath sign, halfway up the next wall. Keep the same direction to cross the next stile then bear right to the bottom of the small wood ahead. Follow the clear path through the trees and at the far side keep the same line across the fields, gradually descending a shallow valley and eventually crossing a farm driveway. Continue ahead but part way across the field bear right to make towards the bottom right-hand corner. The next stile is not obvious but look for two large stones in the hedge a short distance to the left of the field corner. Now bear right across another driveway and cross two wooden stiles close together. Make for a gate straight ahead to reach a road. Continue ahead on the road towards Parwich. In the fields on either side of the road, and at several other places on this walk, you can see the 'ridge and furrow' lines of mediaeval strip farming.

As you enter the village, where the road bends left you pass a footpath on the right showing two miles to Tissington. The walk continues on this path but Parwich is worth a little exploration. It is a secluded, compact little village with a complicated pattern of lanes around two greens. The church was rebuilt in 1872 but retains several fine Norman features. The carving over the tower doorway (called a tympanum) was believed to be Norman but is now thought to be Saxon, possibly 1000 years old. Parwich Hall is conspicuously brick in this otherwise limestone village – a status symbol in 1747, when it was built. Over the bar in the Sycamore Inn hang commemorative footballs from Ashbourne's traditional Shrove Tuesday football game.

From the Sycamore Inn return to the route by turning left just past the pond and continuing past some cottages on a footpath beside a stream, until you emerge with the footpath to Tissington on your left.

Climb the clear path up the fields, from where you get an excellent view of Parwich, and then go down to a footbridge over the Bletch Brook. Continue straight ahead up the hill and on reaching a farm drive turn left along it. At the far side of a bridge over the Tissington Trail turn left and follow a footpath down onto the Trail.

Continue ahead to Tissington station, where you turn right into a road, then left into the village. Tissington is a delightfully unspoilt estate village. Well Dressings are held here at Ascensiontide, with five wells being 'dressed'. The custom is supposed to have started here in the 14th century. The Jacobean Hall has belonged to the Fitzherbert family since the 17th century and the church contains many Norman features and a rare Saxon font.

Tissington Hall and the former village water supply coming from Hall Well

Pass the pond and the old school on your left then turn right and continue past Tissington Hall, opposite which is Hall Well. Keep straight on at the road junction until you reach a sharp left-hand bend where you go through a stile beside a footpath sign on your right.

Following the direction of the signpost cross two fields. In the next field keep straight ahead but parallel to the overhead cables on your left and find a stile just above a farm and some trees. After the next stile continue forward towards Newton Grange Farm but don't go down onto the muddy farm track. Keeping to the contour pass the end of a wire fence and reach a squeezer stile at the field corner. Bear slightly left across a dip in the ground and go around the end of the farm buildings. Bear left to a squeezer stile a little way beyond the farm, in the left-hand corner of the field.

Turn right into the farm road and as it bends left leave it and keep straight forward on a rough track. Immediately before a bridge climb some steps on the right which bring you onto the Trail again. Turn left and follow it back to the car park.

Walk 3:
Ashbourne and Blore

Below the very popular area of Dovedale the valley of the River Dove presents a more gentle, pastoral aspect. This walk is through fields and open parkland, giving wide views over the valley and beyond, and includes a delightful stretch beside the river itself.

An undulating walk, not too strenuous, with several short climbs and one longer, gradual one.

Distance: 8 miles (13km).

Parking: In one of the public car parks in Ashbourne. Map reference 184472.

Map: The Ordnance Survey map most useful on this walk is "Ashbourne and the Churnet Valley (Sheet SK 04/14)" from the Pathfinder series.

From its origins as a mediaeval settlement, mentioned in the Domesday Book, Ashbourne developed as a thriving market town, owing much of its former importance to its position as a meeting place of several coaching routes. The many impressive buildings are testimony to its former standing. Church Street is amongst the finest streets in the county with at one end St Oswald's church, dating back to the 13th century and described as "one of the grandest in Derbyshire". Inside, in the Boothby Chapel, is the famous memorial to Penelope Boothby who died in childhood and whose white marble effigy shows her in a

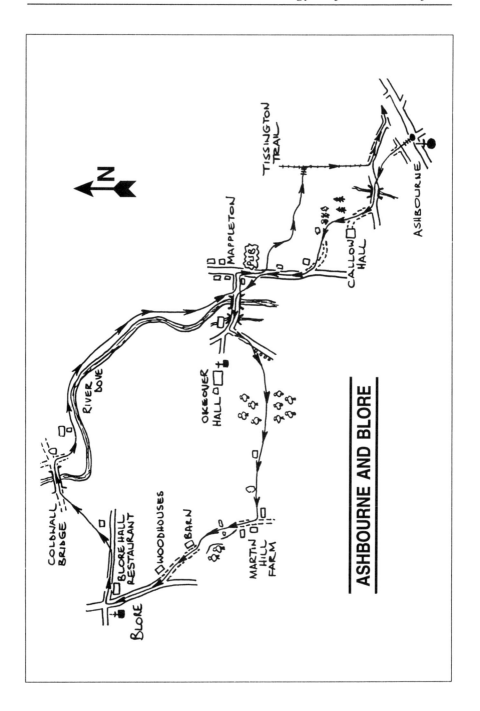

ASHBOURNE AND BLORE

delightful sleeping pose. Depending on where you park you will walk through the town at either the beginning or the end of this walk and so will see many of its interesting historic buildings with their variety of architectural styles.

Start the walk from St Oswald's church. Climb the stepped path called Church Banks which goes up from the main road directly opposite the church gates. Cross the road at the top and continue ahead along a track, soon going through a gate and downhill to emerge into a field. Continue forward over two fields and join a road near a bridge.

Turn left over the bridge and then turn right up Callow Hall drive. Part way up cross the stile on the right and continue uphill beside the fence on your left. Climb steeply past a copse of trees on your left. The tall trees to your right are fine specimens of the Wellingtonia or Big Tree, a form of American Redwood. These can live for over a thousand years and can grow to an enormous size. They occasionally appear in this area in formal parkland settings. Keep straight ahead over the brow of the hill to a stile in a hedge. Cross a large field – the path is not always clear but bear slightly left and make for the farthest left-hand end of a holly hedge, where you cross a stile beside a gate. Now turn left past a gateway and descend the hillside. The path goes close to a farm track, which bends right then left to join the Mappleton road near a house.

Evidence suggests that this road was once part of the route between Derby and Manchester, turnpiked in 1738 and based on an ancient packhorse way. This section was superseded in the 1750s by a shorter route a few miles to the north of Ashbourne. Turn right and follow the road into Mappleton. You will see clearly ahead the distinctive hill called Thorpe Cloud, marking the start of the Dovedale gorge.

Mappleton is a quiet, brick-built village, very different to other settlements further up the Dove Valley, though it is of ancient foundation and has a very unusual 18th century church. But is it Mappleton or Mapleton? The Ordnance Survey, the County Council's road signs and public notices and even local people all offer alternative spellings!

Mappleton Church

Cross the stile opposite the Okeover Arms and bear right over the field to Okeover Bridge and the River Dove. Cross the bridge, then another smaller one over a millstream. A little further along the road, on the right, is the former mill in a very tranquil setting. Turn left onto the unfenced road opposite the mill. Near a set of short stone posts bear right off the road and start to ascend an obvious hollow up the hillside, where the trees are sparse.

Over to your right, as you start to climb, is a fine view of Okeover Hall, built mainly in the 1700s and replacing an earlier house. Additional wings built in the 1950s blend well with the original Georgian structure. The nearby church is not the Victorian estate church which it appears to be but is much older, with features dating from the 14th century.

Okeover Hall

Climb steadily to the top of the hollow and continue straight on, passing a derelict house on your right and aiming for a gap in the trees ahead. Here climb a distinctive metal ladder stile beside a gate and keep on uphill with the wall on your left. Continue forward passing a hedge corner on your left, then skirting a pond and climbing a stile into a narrow walled field immediately before Martin Hill Farm.

At the top of the field go through a gate and turn right to follow the farm track to a gateway beside a large, open barn on the left. Follow the faint path over open fields, keeping to the contour and parallel to the boundary on the left. Pass the scant remains of a barn on your right and continue towards a complete one. Bear left before the barn into a green lane which runs alongside it. Follow this lane to join a metalled road near an unusually styled farmhouse at Woodhouses.

Continue forward along the road, with fine views to Thorpe Cloud and Bunster Hill to your right, to reach the hamlet of Blore. Its full name is Blore Ray, derived from ancient words meaning 'windy place' and is very fitting for its exposed position. The sturdy church, of Norman foundation, is furnished with 16th century oak pews and 17th century box pews. There is also a magnificent alabaster memorial tomb to the Bassett family who inhabited nearby Blore Hall.

At the crossroads just beyond the church turn right, passing Blore Hall, now a restaurant and holiday accommodation, and continue down the road. Cross the next stile on the left, a little way before a farm, and bear right down a large field. Aim a little to the left of the farm and you will eventually reach a stile in the hedge. Continue straight ahead to Coldwall Bridge which can be seen in the valley below.

You may wonder why such a large and well-engineered stone bridge was constructed to carry a farm track over the river. The reason is that when the bridge was built this was no mere farm track but the Blythe Marsh to Thorpe turnpike road, which linked the two main turnpikes leading north from Derby. Look back up the field you have just descended – you can see the line of the former road curving up the hillside. On the other side of the River Dove it climbs steeply up to Thorpe.

At the far side of the bridge the walk turns right onto a track, but before continuing if you go a few yards further on you will see a milestone on the right set up by the Turnpike Trust in 1822. Follow the track as it heads towards a house and cross a stile immediately to the right of the outbuildings. Now continue straight ahead over the fields, at first close to a hedge on the left then close to the river on the right. Follow the obvious route to the road at Okeover Bridge. This is a good stretch for bird spotting – dippers, herons and long-tailed tits are regularly seen.

Turn left and follow the road back into Mappleton. A little way past the Okeover Arms turn left onto a narrow path, signposted to Ashbourne. At the end of the enclosed path cross a stile and bear right up a faint path which becomes clearer as it approaches a gap in the hedge. Keep the same direction, with a hedge on your left, to a footpath sign. Continue beside the hedge on your left to a squeezer stile at the top of the field. Bear slightly right on a clear path to a stile amongst thick bushes. Again follow the hedge on your left over two fields, crossing a farm track on the way.

Continue straight ahead down two more fields and up some steps onto the Tissington Trail. Turn right and walk along the Trail to its end at Mappleton Lane car park. Turn left out of the car park and follow the road into Ashbourne, passing a restored water pump at the corner of Union Street.

Walk 4:
Ashover and the Upper Amber Valley

After climbing to a magnificent viewpoint above the Amber valley the walk continues along quiet lanes and footpaths to pass Ogston Reservoir and return to Ashover along the lower slopes of the valley.

After a long climb at the start the route is fairly easy going.

Distance: *6 miles (10km).*

Parking: *In the public car park by the village hall in Ashover. Map reference 346632.*

Map: *The Ordnance Survey map most useful on this walk is "Chesterfield (sheet SK 36/37)" from the Pathfinder series.*

Ashover, situated in the quiet valley of the River Amber, is an attractive village of fine stone buildings. The church has many interesting features including a lead font, one of only about thirty in the country. Nearby are the ancient Crispin Inn and the former girls' school, now the Parish rooms.

Turn left out of the car park and cross the road to go through a small metal gate at the side of a farm track. Following an obvious path climb gradually up a large field, with a fence on your left as you near the top. Continue up a narrow enclosed path, going under two tunnels, and eventually emerging onto

ASHOVER AND THE UPPER AMBER VALLEY

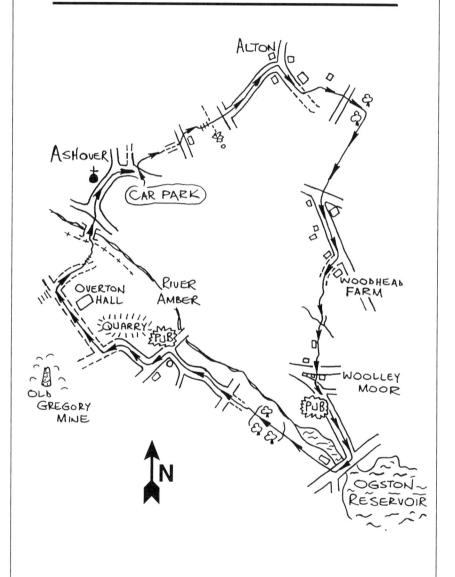

a surfaced lane. Turn left for a short distance, then go through a stile on your right and continue uphill beside a wall on your right. Near the top of the second field turn right through a stile in the wall and continue steeply up some stone steps to heathland at the top of the hill.

The route now lies straight ahead but before continuing it is well worth pausing to explore the gritstone outcrop, a little to the right, known as the Fabric. A nearby view indicator helps identify some of the prominent landmarks of the extensive views. Return to the top of the steps and follow the obvious path ahead and downhill to a road junction. Follow the road to Alton, where you turn right at a T-junction and continue along the road, passing a large farm on your left. Soon after this the road becomes narrower and hollowed.

Look out for a stile, beside a gate, on your left. Cross it and go down the side of a field to climb a stile in the hedge on your right about half way down. Now bear slightly left, making for a point in the hedge opposite, just to the right of a solitary tree, where a stile brings you onto a road. Go over the stile immediately opposite and climb directly up the field, cross a dilapidated wall and continue through the bushes to a stile at the top.

Beyond this turn right and follow the clear path along the edge of the fields close to a hedge and the remains of a wall on your right. Eventually emerge onto a road and continue down Woodhead Lane opposite. After passing two houses on your right you reach Woodhead Farm, where you turn right to go across the farmyard with the farmhouse on your left and on into a hedged track.

Follow this track into a field, where it bends left and becomes open on the right-hand side. Soon it bears right to go through a gateway with a stile alongside. Go through the stile then immediately turn left through a squeezer stile. Walk parallel to the field boundary on your left until as you near the opposite end of the field you bear right to the lower corner of the field. Go over a small stream and through a squeezer stile to continue up into another field. Keep in the same direction to pass a wall corner a little to your right, and come alongside a fence and bushes on your right, behind which is a market garden. Keeping to this boundary go through two stiles, then part way across another field turn sharply right through bushes and then across a stream. Bear left along the edge of a field to reach the road at Woolley Moor.

The route continues along a path directly opposite, between the houses, though before you follow it you might wish to look at the unusual toll cottage a little way along the road to the right. This was the site of the Badger Lane gate, on a branch of the Mansfield to Tibshelf Turnpike. It connected with the Chesterfield to Matlock Turnpike at Kelstedge. At the road beyond the houses turn left, keeping right at the fork, to pass the White Horse pub and continue downhill with a pleasant view of Ogston Reservoir ahead.

Constructed in the late 1950s the reservoir provides facilities for sailing, wind surfing and fishing and is a favoured habitat for a wide variety of birds. At the next road junction turn right crossing a narrow arm of the reservoir (often a good bird spotting point) and go through a stile on the right, immediately beyond a house.

Follow the clear path along the side of fields and through a wood. At the far side of the wood continue straight ahead over two fields and in the third keep to the hedge on your left until you come to a stile beside a gate at the start of an enclosed track. Follow the track to reach a road and continue forward along the minor road opposite. Turn right at the next road junction and walk downhill to Milltown, passing the pinfold on your left.

Follow the road to the left of the Miners' Arms. The pub's
name recalls the heyday of the lead mining industry in this area.
In the late 18th century Milltown had some of the most produc-
tive lead mines in Derbyshire. On reaching a cottage on your
left turn right up another lane, which bends left at the entrance
to a quarry and becomes unsurfaced. On the hillside ahead can
be seen a chimney and other remains of the Gregory Mine
which was one of the largest lead mines in the locality.

Milltown Pinfold

A short way on turn right up another rough track and continue
to pass Overton Hall on your right. This late 17th century house
was for a time the home of Sir Joseph Banks, the famous botanist
who sailed with Captain Cook. Past the hall turn right beside a
large tree into a tree-lined track and where it bears right between stone gateposts go straight ahead over a stile and
through a fence made of stone slabs. These stone 'fences', made

of gritstone slabs probably from local quarries, are a feature of the area. Follow the steps down the field and at the bottom continue forward a short way along a sunken holloway then cross a stile on your left and follow the hedge on your right to another stile.

Now turn left to join a level track which was once part of the line of the Ashover Light Railway. This opened in 1925 and was constructed primarily to carry minerals from the surrounding quarries to Clay Cross Iron Works, although it also ran a limited passenger service. This was the site of the Salter Lane Halt for travellers to and from Ashover village. The line closed in 1950.

The footpath soon bears right off the old railway line and crosses a bridge over the River Amber and continues up a lane to Ashover. Turn left at the top then right up Church Street, past the church and the Crispin Inn, to return to the car park.

Walk 5:
Bakewell and
Great Longstone

*This walk gives sweeping views from the tracks and field paths
linking an old railway line, which forms part of the route, to
Bakewell and the pleasant limestone village of Great
Longstone.*

*After a short, steep climb out of Bakewell the going is easy for
the rest of the walk.*

Distance: *Just over 6 miles (11km).*

Parking: *In one of the car parks in Bakewell.*

Leave Bakewell by the bridge over the River Wye and at the far
end of the bridge turn into the meadow through the small iron
gate on the left. Following the path beside the river go through
two small gates then across a second meadow to reach another
gate onto a minor road. Turn left and walk along the road to a
narrow bridge on your left. The route now turns right up a
rough lane but before you follow it have a look at this 17th
century bridge. It was build for packhorse traffic which, coming
from Bakewell, would have continued up the lane you are about
to follow. Although packhorse bridges are very narrow the low
parapets allowed clearance for the wide loads which the horses
carried. The renovated Holme Bridge Sheepwash at the far side
of the bridge is also worth investigation.

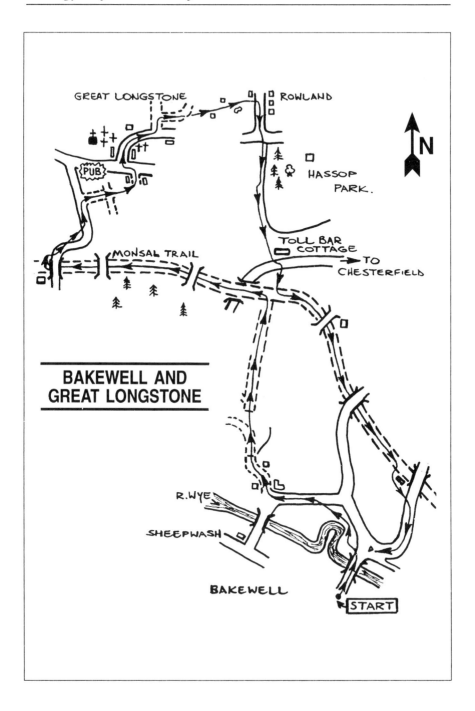

GREAT LONGSTONE

ROWLAND

HASSOP PARK.

PUB

MONSAL TRAIL

TOLL BAR COTTAGE

TO CHESTERFIELD

BAKEWELL AND GREAT LONGSTONE

R.WYE

SHEEPWASH

BAKEWELL

START

Walk up the lane, past an old mine on your right, and go through a gate at the top. Continue up a track, across open grassland, leaving it where it bends sharply left and going straight ahead to another gate at the start of a walled track. Follow the track over the crest of the hill and continue forward. You now have sweeping views of Monsal Head to the left and of Longstone Edge in front. Behind is a wonderful view over Bakewell with its prominent church. Eventually a gate brings you onto the Monsal Trail.

This is the former Bakewell-Buxton branch of the London Midland Railway, closed in 1968 after just over 100 years of operation. Now the track makes a pleasant, easy footpath and provides a favourable habitat for bird and plant life. Turning left follow the Trail until just beyond the third overhead bridge you reach the former Great Longstone station. Some steps on the right up the side of the bridge take you onto the road above.

Turn left along the road and soon go through a stile beside a footpath sign on the left. The clear path bears right across the fields to regain the road through another stile. Turn left and continue along the road as far as a squeezer stile on the right just beyond some modern bungalows. Go along this narrow, surfaced path and pass the school on your left to emerge into the village playing field. Bear left across the corner of the field to a gate and walk down the short lane between cottages to reach the main street beside a butcher's shop.

Almost opposite the shop is Church Lane, signposted to Rowland and Hassop. Follow it past the church on your left and around a right-hand bend. St Giles church is well worth a visit. Some of its original 13th century features remain and it has a particularly fine roof with carvings of flowers and figures. Just beyond a bungalow on the left, turn left up a rough track and very soon turn right along a walled path. When the path turns sharply left go straight ahead through a stile.

Now continue forward across the fields, following the clear path. There is much evidence of old lead-mining activity – disturbed ground and the occasional stone barn – to be seen near the path. Small barns of this type, often found in this part of Derbyshire, were known as 'coes'. Local farmers frequently mined the lead on their land and used the barns both for storing mining tools and sheltering animals. A final stile eventually brings you onto a metalled road at the hamlet of Rowland.

Rowdale Tollhouse

Turn right and walk to the next road junction. Almost opposite is a footpath with the high wall of Hassop Hall on its left. Follow this path, crossing a stile on your right when it is reached, and continuing down the side of the fields, still with the wall on your left. When the wall begins to curve away keep straight ahead making towards a gate to the right of a solitary house. Cross a stile beside the gate and turn left into the road.

The house, now much altered and enlarged, was originally Rowdale Toll House on the Ashford-Baslow turnpike. A toll gate was sited here because of the considerable packhorse traffic coming the way you have come from Rowland or from Bakewell along the track you followed earlier.

Go through the large gate opposite the toll house and cross the field to regain the Monsal Trail. Turn left and follow the Trail back to Bakewell, passing the buildings of Hassop station on the way. At Bakewell station leave the Trail by the path on the right, alongside the nearer end of the imposing station building. Cross the car park diagonally and follow Station Road back into Bakewell.

The former Bakewell Station building

Walk 6:
Bakewell, Over Haddon and Ashford-in-the-Water

Beginning beside the River Wye this route takes you over field paths from a popular market town to one of Derbyshire's beautiful limestone dales, returning through a lovely riverside village.

An undulating walk with several short, steep climbs – though with much easy walking in between. Wellies or walking boots are essential following prolonged rain as the riverside path near Haddon Hall is subject to flooding when the river is very high.

Distance: Just under 9 miles (14km).

Parking: In the public car park on Coombs Road, Bakewell. Map reference 222686.

Leave the car park by the small gate at the end furthest from the road. Turn immediately left and follow the wide track through the showground, with the river to your right. Continue straight ahead on a faint path across a field. Soon after the river comes close to the path you cross a footbridge amongst bushes and turn immediately left to climb a stile into a field. Bear right to join a path running along the contour about half way up the field and follow it to eventually reach a gate into a surfaced lane.

Turn right and almost immediately go left over a metal stile.

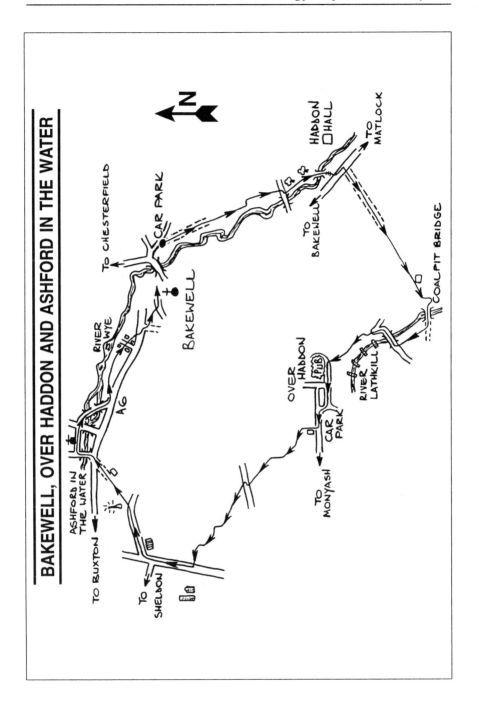

BAKEWELL, OVER HADDON AND ASHFORD IN THE WATER

Now follow the narrow path, beside the river at first and then through the woods of Haddon Park – in which varied and interesting birds and flowers can be found. We have regularly seen great crested grebes, coots, partridges and tree creepers along here and, in season, forget-me-nots, yellow iris and comfrey – the plant much valued by gardeners for composting – make a colourful show. After crossing a footbridge you go uphill and emerge onto the busy A6 road. Turn left and walk on to the entrance to Haddon Hall. The seat of the Duke of Rutland, this has been described as "the finest mediaeval country house in England". The creation of the surrounding park in about 1350 may have led to the disappearance of a nearby village of Nether Haddon.

Cross the road and go through the gate just before the car park. Go straight ahead through another gate and up a rough track, with a wall first on your right then later on your left. Continue to the top of the hill. Looking back you get a fine view of the turrets and battlements of Haddon Hall. Continue straight ahead over several fields, with extensive views all around and often peewits and skylarks for company. After passing close to a cluster of barns on your left keep straight ahead beside a fence, to turn left through a gate at the end of it.

Go forward into the trees and descend a clear path which zig-zags steeply down to the River Lathkill at Coalpit Bridge. This was reputedly the route taken by packhorses bringing coal from the Chesterfield area. A little way beyond the bridge turn right through a stile and follow the obvious path to reach a surfaced road. Turn right and go down the road to cross Conksbury Bridge and continue uphill.

Part way up the hill, where the road bends sharply right, go through a squeezer stile on your left and climb steeply into a field above the trees. Follow the field boundary on your left to a stile then continue on a clear path along the edge of the dale, with an idyllic view of the river below. The way in which the River Lathkill has long been managed for fishing is very clear from up here. Weirs, islands and pools were constructed for rearing trout and increasing the flow of the water to a speed in which they thrive. However, it was not always such a peaceful scene. Lead mining was for many years a local industry and in 1854 there was even a 'gold rush', when gold was supposedly found in one of the mines. The euphoria was very short-lived, though records of that time are unclear as to the reason why – either the quantity of gold found was minute, or it proved to be only iron pyrites or 'fool's gold'.

Coalpit Bridge in Lathkill Dale

Cross a stile on the right over a fence and an obvious path takes you over two fields to the road beside the Lathkill Dale Hotel. Beyond the pub follow the road straight ahead through Over Haddon village, bearing right as you approach the village car park. Turn left at a T-junction and continue along the Monyash road. Just past a house on your right turn right over a stile immediately before a barn. Climb beside a wall on your left and bear left after crossing a stile at the top of the field. Bear right after the next stile to the top left-hand corner of a field and find a stile close to a water trough. Keep the same direction over the next field then turn right with a wall close on your right. After the next stile cross two fields diagonally to reach a surfaced road.

Walk a few steps to your right and cross a stile opposite, just beyond a tree. Bear left up the field on a faint path, cross a stile and keep the same direction over two more fields. Then follow the boundary on your right around the next field to a stile over the fence on the right about half way along the opposite side. Bear left over the next field, passing a footpath sign, and cross a stile on the right at the corner of a small wood. A few yards further on, turn left between walls to emerge at the top of a steep field above Kirk Dale. On the opposite hill can be seen the prominent remains of the Magpie Mine – which finally closed in 1958, bringing to an end 300 years of lead mining on the site. The main shaft was 600 feet deep and a three-mile-long tunnel, or sough, drained water from the mine into the River Wye.

Go straight downhill to a stile by a gate and turn right down the road. Just after passing a left turn to Sheldon bear right up another road. The decaying wooden structure on the right is probably a loading platform for the nearby disused quarry. Continue along the road until you come level with a TV relay mast. Go through a gate on your left and follow the clear path steeply downhill beside a wall. Where the wall bends right go straight ahead, past a line of trees and then a house on your right. Follow a rough track downhill and onto the A6 road.

Cross the road and go over the Sheepwash Bridge into Ashford-in-the-Water. In summer the sheepwash at the side of this

The weirs in Lathkill Dale

beautiful 17th century bridge is occasionally still used for its original purpose. Nearby a particular form of dark limestone was quarried which, when polished, was known as Ashford 'marble'. Examples of this can be seen in the church, together with several preserved 'funeral garlands' – decorations carried in the funeral processions of young girls.

Turn right to pass the church and follow the road through the village to the junction with a main road, opposite the cricket pitch. Cross the main road and go straight ahead past the cricket pitch on your left and over two bridges. On reaching the A6 go through a small gate on your left and follow the obvious path beside the river. Eventually the path bears right away from the river and becomes enclosed between houses. Cross a road and continue ahead to regain the main Bakewell to Buxton road.

Here you can turn left and follow the road back to the centre of Bakewell.

However, for a quieter, if rather more strenuous route, walk a little way to the left along the road then cross it to the start of a rough track. Here climb a clear path on the left up a wooded slope to the top of the hill where it levels out and bears right around the edge of a school sports field. On reaching a road, turn left and follow it downhill into Bakewell.

Walk 7:
Barlow

Some of the many field paths and old lanes which connect farms and hamlets provide an interesting and varied walk around a largely unspoilt and peaceful valley. A particular feature is the rich variety of plants and fungi to be seen in season.

An undulating walk with no strenuous gradients.

Distance: 6 miles (10km).

Parking: On the roadside near Barlow Church.
Map reference 345746.

From the church walk past the vicarage and Church Farm and where the road bends left go forward into a narrow surfaced lane and continue straight ahead to eventually cross a brook at Lee Bridge. Immediately beyond the bridge turn right on a clear path through the trees. Continue over the fields to reach the hamlet of Fender, at the junction of several rough tracks. A railway line used to run from here down the valley towards Chesterfield taking coal from several small collieries in the area and a tramway connected it to workings on the hill above. The route of the railway can still be clearly seen.

Take the wide track, almost opposite, to Monkwood, marked as a private road. Beyond Monkwood Farm the track bears left and nearby, on the left, is a stone bearing the date 1908. This is one of several similar stones in the wood recording when sections were felled and replanted. Ignore any side paths and follow the wide track to a stile and a gate at the end of the wood.

Continue forward and at Lees Common Farm go through the small gate and immediately turn left over a stile. Go straight down the field, over a footbridge and up through trees to cross another field and a stile onto a minor road. Turn left and follow the road around a sharp right-hand bend and uphill to pass through Barlow Lees. Records show that the impressive Lees

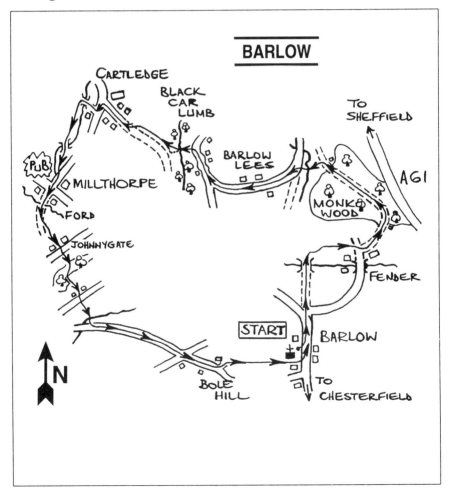

Hall Farm has existed since at least the 15th century. Carry on, eventually going downhill to a road junction, where you turn right. Walk past a group of houses and just beyond them when the road climbs to a right-hand bend turn left through a stile on a footpath signposted to Holmesfield.

Lees Hall Farm, Barlow Lees

Descend steeply to a footbridge over the stream in Black Carr Lumb. Beyond it bear sharply right up through the trees to a stile over a fence and continue forward to the edge of a large field. Following a clear path cross the field diagonally, passing beneath overhead cables, and climb the step stile in the corner of the field. Climb the next field with the hedge on your left. The next (very modern squeezer-type!) stile brings you to the junction of an old lane and a newer farm track. Go through a gate on your left and forward up the lane to Cartledge, where a group of farms and cottages surround the Hall, itself a fine example of a local 15th century yeoman's house.

On reaching Millthorpe Lane turn left down the road and almost immediately turn right onto a footpath signposted to Unthank. Follow the obvious path until just beyond a foot-bridge you turn left in the direction of Millthorpe. Keep roughly parallel to the bushes on your left and at the bottom of the second field bear left and cross a footbridge. Turn right and continue, now with bushes on your right, and eventually emerge into Millthorpe Lane again.

Walk down to the crossroads at Millthorpe and continue ahead down Mill Lane to a ford and a footbridge. Nothing now remains of the mill which stood just upstream from the ford and was an important site in the valley, giving the hamlet its name. Cross the stream and a short way beyond climb a stile on your left and follow the hedge on the right to another footbridge. Beyond it bear right to climb two fields and pass between a house and a barn onto a minor road.

Cross the stile almost opposite (signposted to Oxton Rakes) and bear left past a barn to follow the hedge on your left to Broadmeadow Wood. Bear right to follow a clear path through the trees and continue across fields and up a hill to a farmyard, beyond which you reach a surfaced road. Climb the stile oppo-site and go straight downhill. When the hedge on your left bears left near the bottom go straight forward through the bushes. Cross a footbridge and climb to a surfaced road.

Turn left up the road and continue for some distance, keeping straight on at a crossroads to the top of Bole Hill. Turn left into a driveway at a footpath sign then almost immediately go right, through two gates and into a field. Bole Hill is a common place-name in Derbyshire and usually indicates an ancient lead-smelting site. Open windy hilltops such as this provided plenty of draught to draw the furnace and disperse the poisonous fumes.

The path now goes straight ahead beside the hedge on your right. Towards the end of the field bear left across the corner to a step stile. Now keep straight ahead over the fields via stiles and gateways, making towards Barlow Church. The church is of Norman foundation and the Victorian rebuilders retained several original features. The outside stairway once led to a gallery. Continue, with the churchyard wall on your left, around a farmyard to return to your starting point.

Barlow Church

Walk 8:
Carsington Water,
Hognaston and Brassington

Following quiet lanes and less popular footpaths this walk links four pleasant villages set in a gentle landscape.

A moderately strenuous walk but with no severe gradients.

Distance: *8 miles (13km).*

Parking: *Sheepwash car park, Carsington Water.*
Map reference 249529.

From the far end of the car park follow the way-marked foot-path, with the reservoir on your left. The sensitive planning and management of this recently established reservoir are very evident along this stretch. New planting blends well with the original landscape and a wide variety of plants and birds can be seen. When you reach the newly planted area at the approach to the Visitors Centre look out for an inconspicuous step-stile over a fence on your right. Go straight ahead up two fields, bear slightly left across a third and keep the same direction to a stile, by a footpath sign, which brings you to a road.

Cross the road and climb the stile almost opposite. Go straight forward beside a hedge on your left, through another stile and then continue ahead to reach a farm lane. Turn left and follow the lane to just beyond Overtown Farm where you bear right to a stile and a gate. Go through the stile and walk down a large

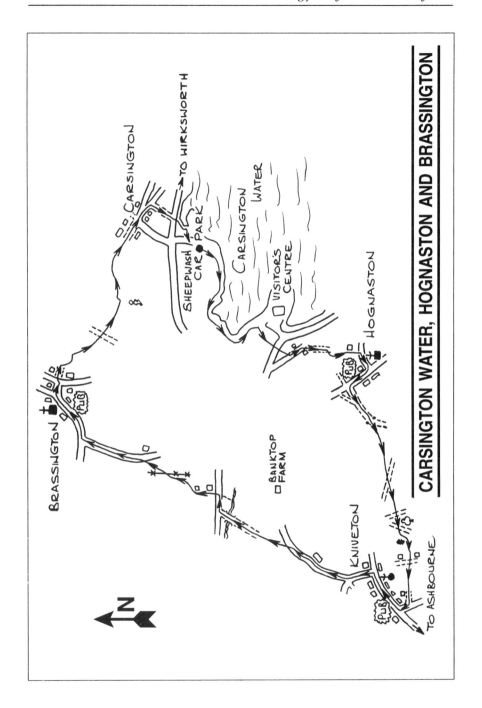

field with a hedge on your right. At the bottom a stile takes you into a green lane – which is often muddy.

Follow the lane until you come to a small bridge and a stile on your right. Go over this and then continue close to the hedge on your left over two fields to a further stile. Keep straight ahead through a gap in a sparse hedge, then make for the right-hand side of a house at the bottom of the field. Go through a small metal gate at the side of the house (the first of many such gates you will see on this walk) to reach a lane which brings you into Hognaston between the church and the former village bakery. The church tower is 15th century and has walls 5 feet thick, but the most notable feature of the church is, perhaps, the well preserved carving of the tympanum over the doorway in the porch.

Hognaston Church

Turn right up the main street, pass the Red Lion pub and continue to almost the end of the houses where you turn left at a footpath sign onto a rough track. Keep on uphill past several houses and the junction with another track. Continue until you reach two large stone posts where the track crosses a small stream. Beyond this the track bears slightly left and goes downhill to a farm but you bear slightly right off it, climbing gradually up a large field and making for a stile and a gate in the hedge at the top.

Go straight ahead to the next stile then bear slightly left on a faint path to a further stile beside a gate. Cross a farm track and keep the same direction to a small metal gate on the far side of the field, just before some trees. These distinctive little gates – perhaps made locally – seem to be a functional alternative to stiles in this area. Continue over another track and onto a signposted footpath through a copse of young trees. Cross yet another track and go forward through two more metal gates and into a field.

The path ahead is not easily found but follow the fence on your left a short way then bear right around a rough hollow and bushes and make for a thick hedge which goes downhill. Descend the field with this hedge on your left, turn left through a gateway at the bottom and continue in the same direction, with a wall now close on your right. Eventually you reach a rough track beside a derelict building.

Cross the track and go through the gate opposite. Keeping to the right of and above a stream you now walk downhill, parallel to Kniveton's main street, crossing two fields to eventually reach a metal gate beside a yew tree. This brings you onto a narrow path, then a metalled road and finally to the main road through Kniveton near the village pump.

Tucked away between hills Kniveton is a delightful little

village. The tiny church is very plain and one of its remaining Norman features, discovered in 1842, is a crudely carved crucifix on a round stone, now set in a wall inside. Evidence suggests that the main road through Kniveton may have been part of the Roman road, known as Hereward Street, which linked a fort at Rocester, in Staffordshire, with another at Chesterfield.

Turn right and walk up the main road past the Red Lion and the church, then immediately before the Village Hall turn left onto a road. Follow the road until it bends left near the entrance to a caravan site. Here bear right onto a pleasant country lane. Keep straight on, ignoring a left turn, to pass Newhouse Farm and an underground reservoir at the top of the hill. Soon after this the lane bears right, becoming a private road. You bear left and continue on a clear track beside a fence on your left. The track becomes hollowed and eventually brings you to a minor road. Turn right along it for a little way to the second footpath sign on the left, immediately before a farm.

Cross the stile and bear right to follow a narrow (often muddy) path up through bushes beside a fence and into a field. Continue straight uphill to turn right through a stile immediately beyond Crowstones Farm. Now bear slightly left to find a stile above a wide hollow. Beyond this the path is not always clear but bear left to follow the overhead power lines and the next stile is just above the point where the lines cross the hedge. Keep straight ahead over the next field going under the power lines then passing a solitary tree a little to your left. Go through a gate and continue forward to join a surfaced farm track near a stone barn.

Turn left onto the track and follow it, as it becomes tarmac, to reach Brassington. Turn right at a road junction, by the curious house formerly called the Tinderbox, and walk through the village. Brassington is a village of grey stone perched on a green hillside, once a thriving centre of the lead mining industry, and has many good 18th century houses. The sturdy church dates from the 11th or early 12th century and one of its few original features is the 'oldest inhabitant of Brassington' – a roughly carved figure of a man high up on the inside of the tower. The Gate Inn probably takes its name from a turnpike toll-gate sited nearby. The ancient road from Derby to Manchester followed a Roman road for much of its length and passed through Brassington. It was turnpiked in 1738, mainly to ensure its improvement.

The Gate Inn, Brassington

Just beyond the church turn right to pass the Miners Arms, which has associations with the lead mining industry. At the next road junction go straight across in front of the Dragon House onto a signposted footpath. A little to the right, across the road, is the Tudor House with a date stone of 1615.

At the end of the farmyard go through a stile on your right and follow the clear path. After crossing two fields turn left to climb steeply then turn right through a wall and climb more gradually through old lead workings. Continue over the hill and down into a shallow valley. The obvious path crosses a track and continues up the opposite side. At the top bear left, to cross the remains of a wall, then right and descend to a stile by a gate, now with a magnificent view of Carsington Water. Beyond the gate the path becomes a wide track and finally a surfaced lane between houses, bringing you to a road junction in Carsington.

Follow the road straight ahead then bear right at the fork to pass the village green and the remains of a cross on your left. Just before reaching the school turn right up a lane which brings you to the main road. Cross it and follow the way-marked footpath back to the car park.

Walk 9:
Carsington Water and
Kirk Ireton

Pleasant field paths link a scenic new reservoir with a nearby village.

An easy walk with only gentle gradients.

Distance: *3.5 miles (5km).*

Parking: *Millfields car park, Carsington Water.*
Map reference 246500.

Planned during the 1960s to increase water supplies to the East Midlands, Carsington Water now blends into its rural setting and provides a most attractive amenity for the region. Whilst offering impressive facilities for water sports, great care has been taken to encourage and safeguard wildlife. The extensive planting of native trees and shrubs around the slopes blends well with existing features and provides excellent opportunities for bird watching.

Leave Millfields car park, with Carsington Water on your left, along the yellow-way-marked footpath which follows the contours of the land around the reservoir. The path runs close to the water and eventually brings you into the surfaced Oldfields Lane near Waterside Cottages (formerly Upperfield Farm). The sensitive blending of newly planted areas with old copses can be clearly seen along the way.

Turn right and walk up the lane, past New Buildings Farm on the left, to a T-junction by a house. Cross the road and climb a stile into a field. Go straight ahead to the next stile amongst holly bushes a little to the left of the field corner. Now continue forward over two fields, then bear slightly right over two more. The clear path then becomes fenced between houses and emerges into the road at Kirk Ireton. Turn right and follow the road to the centre of the village.

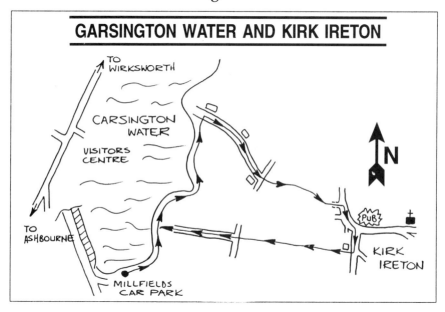

GARSINGTON WATER AND KIRK IRETON

An attractive, well-kept little village, Kirk Ireton is worth exploring. The Barley Mow Inn must be one of the most unusual and inconspicuous pubs for many miles around! The building is a fine example of late Derbyshire Jacobean, built in 1683. The church has several features indicating its Norman origins and is approached through an 18th century gateway which reputedly came from a former manor house. The wall of the squat, low tower has iron bracing below the clock face, as a result of a day in 1811 when a great gale blew away the tower roof.

Take the road signposted to Blackwell and Hulland, which leaves the main street almost opposite the Barley Mow. A short distance along, where the road forks, turn right through a stile. Keep straight ahead now, across the fields. The path is not always evident but the route is clearly marked with stiles. A final stile beside a tall wooden pole brings you onto a road.

Go straight across and continue down Hays Lane. Now Carsington Water and its surrounds comes once more into view. Part way down the lane you pass the entrance to Riddings nursery. At the bottom of the lane turn left and follow the way-marked path back to the car park.

The Barley Mow, Kirk Ireton

Walk 10:
Chatsworth Park and
Ball Cross

Before returning along the popular riverside walk through Chatsworth Park this route takes you through some quieter but equally enjoyable parts of the estate.

Mostly easy walking with just two short climbs.

Distance: Just under 6 miles (9km).

Parking: The car park at Calton Lees (near Chatsworth Garden Centre).
Map reference 258685.

From the car park pass the entrance to the Garden Centre and continue along the lane to reach Calton Lees. Where the lane bends left go straight ahead through a gate and follow the rough track with a small stream on your left. In late summer many half-grown pheasants, bred to stock the Chatsworth Estate, frequent this area. The track eventually zig-zags steeply upwards, passing through Calton Houses to a gate beyond the hamlet. Through the gate follow the path uphill with the wall close on your right.

At the top of the hill follow the clear path across the pasture towards a plantation. Some distance to the right, not on a public path, is the decorated wooden house sent to the 6th Duke of Devonshire by his friend Tsar Nicholas I in 1855 and known as

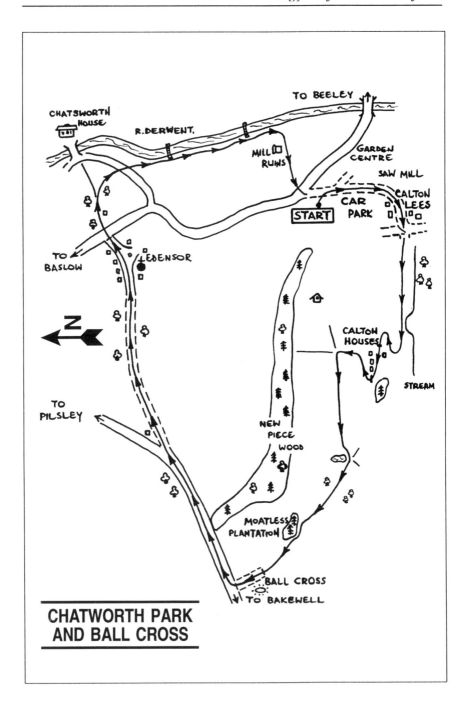

**CHATWORTH PARK
AND BALL CROSS**

Russian Cottage. Half-way to the plantation a track crosses the path. Turn left along the track, towards Ball Cross and Bakewell, and continue to a step-stile beside a gate.

Beyond the stile keep straight ahead, parallel to a fence a little to your left at first, then, near the end of the large field, move closer to the fence and eventually cross it via a step-stile. Bear right to skirt the end of a pond, cross another stile and continue in the direction shown for Ball Cross. The path is not always clear but aim for the small hill with trees on top, bearing left up the hill on a clearer path which joins a level track. Continue in the same direction, with the Moatless Plantation on your right and soon descend to a stile beside a gate, taking you into a

Guide 'stoop' near Edensor

walled track. To the left is the site of the Iron Age fort of Ball Cross. This was probably the stronghold of a local chieftain, rather than a defence for an important pre-historic route, as Mam Tor and Fin Cop forts were.

At the end of the track you come to a minor road. This steep, narrow road was constructed in 1810 to replace the even steeper packhorse route between Bakewell and Chesterfield, the worn 'holloways' of which can be seen in the field and woods to the left. Eventually the '13 bends' of the present A619 made a longer but much easier route between the two towns.

Turn right and walk along the road, over the crest of the hill, past a small wood on the left to eventually turn right onto an unsurfaced lane. In the angle of the road junction is a four-sided stone pillar. This 'signpost' (see photograph on previous page) was erected in 1709 in response to an Act of Parliament saying that such guidestones must be set up along the old trade routes. There are numerous others remaining in Derbyshire, many with similarly carved pointing hands showing the way to the nearest market towns, in this instance Bakewell, Chesterfield and Sheffield. The 'Chesterfield Rode' is the rough lane you follow down the hill.

One of Edensor's eccentric architectural styles

Part way down the lane, to the left, is a picture postcard view of Chatsworth, with the spire of Edensor church in the foreground. Continue into Edensor village – a curious collection of architectural styles including Norman, Tudor and Italianate. The present village was built by the sixth Duke to replace the original which spoilt the view from Chatsworth House! Pass the church, go through a gate and cross the main road to continue along the path opposite. On the right is the only house remaining of the former Edensor village.

As you pass through some trees turn right off the path, cross the driveway of Chatsworth House and aim straight downhill to the River Derwent. On reaching the well-worn path beside the river follow it downstream to the ruins of Chatsworth Mill. Just beyond the mill turn right and climb to a gate leading back to the car park.

Walk 11:
Derwent Edge

*A high-level moorland walk, offering spectacular views, which
begins and ends beside the impressive dams of the upper
Derwent Valley.*

*A strenuous walk involving a long steep climb onto Derwent
Edge. As much of the route is over open moorland
inexperienced walkers should only attempt it in clear weather.*

Distance: *Just under 9 miles (14km).*

Parking: *Fairholmes car park.
Map reference 172893.*

The car park from which this walk starts is sited where Fairholmes Farm stood when this was a secluded valley of scattered
farms. A tremendous change took place between 1901 and 1916
when the Howden and Derwent reservoirs were built to meet
the region's increasing need for water. Ladybower reservoir
was constructed between 1935 and 1945, when the villages of
Ashopton and Derwent were submerged beneath its waters.

Turn right from the car park and follow the road below the
massive wall of the Derwent Dam and on up the opposite side
of the valley to level out with Ladybower reservoir on the right.
Keep to this road (the only stretch of road remaining from
before the valley was flooded), passing several houses, a telephone box and the former village school.

Just before the road dips to cross Mill Brook you pass a pair

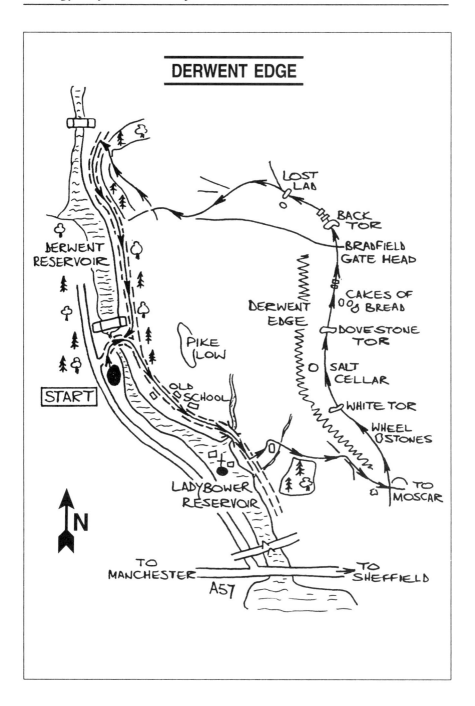

DERWENT EDGE

LOST LAD

BACK TOR

BRADFIELD GATE HEAD

DERWENT RESERVOIR

CAKES OF BREAD

DERWENT EDGE

DOVESTONE TOR

PIKE LOW

SALT CELLAR

WHITE TOR

START

OLD SCHOOL

WHEEL STONES

LADYBOWER RESERVOIR

TO MOSCAR

N

TO MANCHESTER

TO SHEFFIELD

A57

of large stone gateposts on the right. These mark one of the entrances to Derwent Hall which, together with the church and other buildings in the village of Derwent, was demolished when the reservoir was built. The church spire was left intact for some years and showed above the water when the level was low. However, it was finally blown up, for safety reasons, after people tried to swim out to it during periods of drought.

The road becomes unsurfaced and soon, immediately after the entrance to Ashes Farm, cross the stile on your left, signposted to Derwent Edge and Moscar. Like several similar footpath signs in the area this indicates an old-established route out of the valley. This was a 'jaggers' road for packhorses which crossed a bridge in Derwent and climbed over the moors towards Sheffield.

Climb the field then follow the field boundary on your left up to Grindle Barn – which bears the date 1647. Turn right around the end of the barn and follow the clear track to soon cross the stream in Grindle Clough. Pass through a gateway and climb the obvious track beside the wall on your right. The track continues past a plantation, now with the wall on the left, to reach a gate. Beyond this bear right over bracken-covered open ground and go through a further gate onto a level track.

Turn right and follow the track with the wall close on your right and soon turn left up an obvious grassy path. It becomes stony and eventually passes a cairn before reaching a signpost near a shooting butt at a footpath crossroads on top of the ridge.

Now turn left and follow the well-worn path along Derwent Edge, enjoying the magnificent views. A succession of fantastically weathered gritstone outcrops mark the route, including the curious Salt Cellar (just off the track on the left) and the Cakes of Bread. Soon after Dovestone Tor the route crosses a boggy area but look ahead for the stone slabs which eventually provide welcome assistance as well as protecting the moorland from continuing erosion. Despite their almost artificial appearance these, we are told, are flagstones from the floors of derelict Lancashire mills – 'helicoptered' to the hills in large bundles. Just before the prominent trig point on Back Tor is reached the route crosses the Abbey Grange to Strines footpath at Bradfield Gate Head.

Helena Russel

The Salt Cellar, Derwent Edge

From Back Tor the path bears slightly left over another boggy area and crosses a slight dip before climbing to a cairn and a view indicator on top of Lost Lad. The name of this hill (which gives some of the best views of the walk) refers to the story of a 16th century shepherd boy from Derwent who perished in a blizzard hereabouts. His body was reputedly found the following spring under a boulder on which were scratched the words 'lost lad' and beneath which he had tried to find shelter.

Go straight on down the other side of the hill, keeping left when the path forks and then following the wide grassy path, which bends to the left. Continue ahead to eventually cross a derelict wall by a stone post and go forward to climb a ladder stile over a fence. Now follow the wall on your right until another wall is reached. Turn left before the wall, as shown by a marker post, and go downhill beside the wall to a footpath crossroads sign.

Turn right through the heather, towards Abbey Bank and Howden Dam, on a clear path which soon descends to continue beside a wall. After a while you drop steeply downhill beside a deep holloway and the dam of the Howden reservoir suddenly comes into view ahead. On reaching the wall above a plantation turn left through a gateway and follow the obvious path through the trees, to join the track beside the Derwent reservoir. In spring, masses of daffodils bloom here, wild remnants of the garden of the vanished Abbey Farm.

Turn left and walk back along the track to the Derwent Dam. The Howden and Derwent dams were used in the preparation for an air-strike on German dams in the Second World War, using the new 'bouncing bomb'. The story of this mission was told in the film "The Dambusters". Just before you reach the dam wall cross a stile on your right to follow the path down through the trees and regain the road below the dam. Retrace your steps to the car park.

Walk 12:
Edale and Rushup Edge

A high-level ridge walk giving extensive views over the Edale and Hope Valleys and far beyond.

A fairly strenuous walk involving several steep climbs.

Distance: *6.5 miles (10.5km).*

Parking: *In the public car park at Edale.*
Map reference 124854.

Turn left out of the main exit of the car park and walk a little way along the road, crossing a stream, to a footpath on the right, signposted to Hollins Cross and Castleton. Follow this farm track over the River Noe and up the hillside. Until 1633, when a chapel was built in Edale, funeral processions came up this 'coffin road' to the church at Castleton. A short distance beyond some barns bear right off the track and continue on a very clear signposted path to climb steadily to Hollins Cross. This route over the ridge was the way workers from Castleton walked daily to and from Edale Mill. The mill itself, now converted to flats, can be seen below, a little further down the Edale valley.

Turn right at Hollins Cross and follow the well-worn path along the ridge to the summit of Mam Tor. Here you can clearly see the earthworks which formed the largest Iron Age fort in the Peak District. Its strategic position, guarding an important trade route dating from pre-historic times, can be fully appreciated. The views from here are extensive though several of the

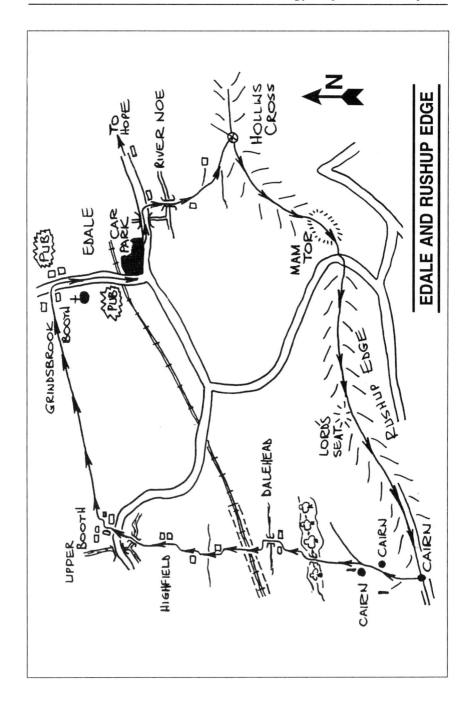

EDALE AND RUSHUP EDGE

region's large quarries are clearly visible scars on the impressive natural scenery. The landscape illustrates perfectly the continuing conflict between the need to secure employment for local people whilst maintaining the area's natural beauty. Continue down the far side of Mam Tor and on reaching the minor road at Mam Nick turn left and walk a few paces down the road. Cross a stile on the right and continue on another very prominent path up onto Rushup Edge.

Continue ahead along the ridge with a wall on your left, climbing gradually and eventually reaching the highest point at Lords Seat – an unusually large Bronze Age burial mound. Keep straight ahead until you reach a footpath signpost and cairn, just before the path becomes enclosed by walls. Here turn right onto another equally obvious path. This is Chapel Gate, the old road going between the Edale Valley and Chapel-en-le-Frith. It is a good illustration of the standard of road which linked communities in the days before turnpiking started·improvements, which gradually established the network of surfaced roads we now take for granted.

Follow the path past a cairn to reach a footpath sign, a wooden post and another cairn close together, just before the path begins to go downhill. A few paces beyond the sign turn left off the main path in the direction shown for Dalehead and Upper Booth. The steep path is not very clear at first but aim on a line between the left-hand end of the first line of trees below and the farm a little way beyond. The path becomes clear lower down. At the bottom of the hill cross a small wooden bridge and bear right up the opposite bank to climb a step stile over a wall.

Now bear left over the field to a wooden stile and keep the same direction to the next stile. Then continue to reach the left-hand end of the buildings at Dalehead and turn right through the gate. The farther end of the building, houses a small shelter providing information about the area. Turn immediately left past this to climb a stile then cross a footbridge over a small stream. Turn left again to follow a wire fence on your right to a stile beside the gate ahead. The stone construction you pass is an air shaft for the Cowburn Tunnel, which takes the Sheffield-Manchester railway line between Edale and Chinley.

A quiet corner at Upper Booth

Continue ahead over two more stiles then bear left to skirt Orchard Farm. Climb a ladder stile, cross a tiny stream then keep straight ahead to come alongside a wall and fence on your right and go through a gate into a farmyard. Bear right around the barn to another gate into a field. Go straight forward past an electricity pole then bear right to a small gate on the left of some barns. Follow the footpath signposted to Upper Booth, climb a stile over a wall and continue in the same direction, keeping on the contour and passing a line of trees on your right. At the end of the field go through a squeezer stile and down through trees to cross a footbridge over the Crowden Brook and emerge onto a surfaced road at Upper Booth. The several hamlets or 'booths' of the Edale valley were recorded in 16th and 17th century documents as simple shelters for herdsmen, shepherds and their animals.

Cross the road and continue up a farm track, signposted to Edale and Grindsbrook Booth. This is part of the alternative route of the Pennine Way and is easily followed across the fields. Recent work to combat erosion testifies to the popularity of walking in the Edale valley!

When you reach Grindsbrook Booth turn right into the road and continue down it to the car park.

Walk 13:
Eyam Moor

This walk climbs the hill above the 'Plague Village' of Eyam, giving panoramic views, then passes through a secluded valley before returning over heather-covered moorland.

Mostly easy walking apart from a steep climb at the start and a more gradual one on the return.

Distance: *Just over 6 miles (10km).*

Parking: *The car park at Hawkhill Road, Eyam. Map reference 216767.*

In 1665, a box of tailor's cloth sent from plague-ridden London brought the deadly germs to the village of Eyam. The disease spread rapidly and within about fifteen months five out of every six of the inhabitants had died. The local clergymen persuaded the villagers to stay in the village, despite their instinctive desire to flee, and thus the plague was contained within Eyam. The houses of many of the victims, their graves and other memorials can be seen throughout the village.

Turn right out of the car park up Hawkhill Road and take the first turn left up a surfaced 'no-through-road' which soon becomes a stony enclosed track. There are good views over Eyam and the wider area which become more and more extensive as you climb to eventually reach a metalled road. Turn left and follow the road for some distance. From here the enormous impact on the landscape of the local industry of limestone

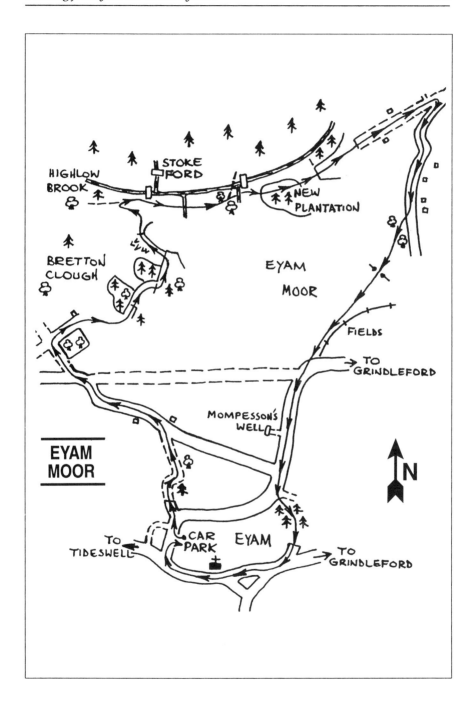

quarrying is very evident. Further along the road a totally different view is presented of unspoilt gritstone moors.

At the second sharp bend a rough track joins the road. A short distance past this junction turn right along a second rough track. Immediately beyond a small wood, climb a stile on your right and walk along the edge of the wood. Follow the clear path beside a wall on your left. When a small shed is reached bear slightly right across the field to continue on a grassy, walled track immediately to the right of a wood. After crossing a stile the track becomes walled only on the left and brings you to another stile beside a gate among some trees. Cross this stile and turn left to continue with the wall still on the left.

The path is quite clear as it descends gradually below a heather-clad hillside to reach a wooden stile beside a gate at the junction of two walls. Here is a superb view over Bretton Clough. In this secluded wooded valley and the adjoining Abney Clough local people supposedly hid themselves and their cattle from the army of Bonnie Prince Charlie on his march towards Derby in 1745. Climb the stile and continue, with the wall on your right, along the obvious path on the edge of a gritstone outcrop, to a ladder stile. Now descend more steeply following a well-worn path which soon bears left and later sharply right and becomes deeply hollowed as it approaches the stream at Stoke Ford. At this pleasant spot several ancient routes crossed the Highlow and Bretton Brooks.

Don't cross the bridge but bear right to climb slightly and follow a clear path above the stream. The path levels out for a little way before it drops again to cross a tiny stream and climbs through a derelict wall. Now continue more or less on the level with superb views over Hathersage to Carl Wark, Higger Tor and Stanage Edge. Descend through trees and just before reaching a ford and footbridge bear right across the small stream which runs into the Highlow Brook. Cross a stile and continue ahead through a new plantation to reach a gate into a field. Keep near the boundary wall of a wood on your left until it turns downhill, where you go straight ahead. Go through a gate and keep in the same direction along a farm track. Pass between a farm and an open shed and finally reach a metalled road.

Turn right and walk up the road, around two sharp bends and continue past Leam Farm until you come to two large barns. Climb a stile on the right, signposted to Sir William Road. The obvious path climbs gradually bringing you onto Eyam Moor. Part way across the moor you reach a wire fence on your left which you follow until you cross a stile onto a road.

Continue ahead along the metalled road and after going over a slight rise you pass Mompesson's Well on your right. This spring is named after William Mompesson, the Rector of Eyam at the time of the Plague. Food and other necessities for the village were left at points such as this on the village boundaries and the money for payment was 'disinfected' by leaving it in vinegar or running water. Shortly after the well is a road

Saxon cross in Eyam churchyard

junction and just beyond it you go through a stile on your left, at the start of a wood. Follow the obvious path down through the wood and continue on the metalled lane between the houses below. Keep on downhill until you reach the main street.

Turn right and walk back through the village to the car park. You will pass many interesting features of the village such as the Bull Ring, the church (with its reminders of the Plague), the stocks and the old market hall.

Walk 14:
Matlock Bath and Bonsall

Following an old route high above the bustle of Matlock Bath this walk takes you to the former lead-mining village of Bonsall, then back over Masson Hill by way of leadminers' paths and tracks. It gives extensive views and an unusual perspective of Matlock and Matlock Bath.

Although not very long, this walk starts with a very steep climb and also includes two rather less strenuous ones.

Distance: *Just over 4 miles (7km).*

Parking: *Matlock Bath Station.*
Map reference 298584.

Matlock Bath, where the River Derwent runs through a deep limestone gorge, has long been popular with visitors to Derbyshire. The Romans came to mine lead; the thermal springs provided 'hydrotherapy' for wealthy visitors in the 18th and 19th centuries and modern attractions include the riverside illuminations in the autumn and the cable car ride across the gorge.

From the car park cross the river and the A6 and go up Holme Road, immediately opposite. As you climb steadily, ignoring side roads, a wonderful view over the roofs of the town is gradually revealed. Continue on Upperwood Road to pass a former toll house on your left – known as "The Threepenny Bit" from its distinctive shape. It was built around the end of the

18th century, probably to collect tolls from packhorses bringing lead along this roadway from mines in the hills above. A short way beyond the entrance to the Heights of Abraham turn right up a narrow waymarked path beside a house.

The Threepenny Bit house high above Matlock Bath

The path is stepped in places and climbs steeply through the trees. Keep straight on and eventually emerge at the top of the wood at a footpath sign near Ember Farm. Go through the stile on the left and bear right onto a farm track, in the direction shown for Bonsall. Follow this lane until it descends to reach the village opposite the church. The church is perched prominently above the village and has a distinctive spire with ornamental bands. Inside is a 17th century funeral helmet. Turn right and walk down Church Lane to the old market place with its thirteen-stepped cross and the Kings Head pub which dates from 1677.

Bonsall was long associated with lead mining, which ac-

The market cross at Bonsall

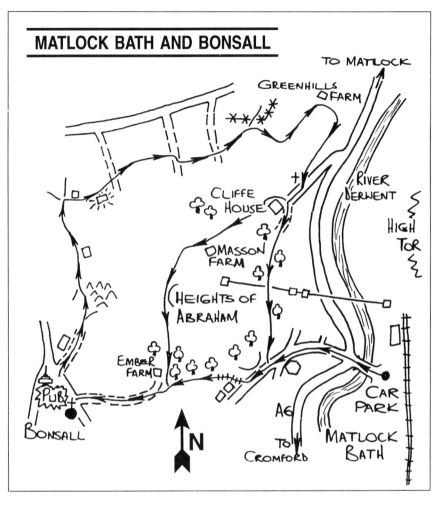

counts for the extensive network of paths surrounding the village. Continue up the lane leading from the top of the market place, passing a telephone box on your left. Framework knitting was another local industry and just above the telephone box you pass a remaining framework shop with large windows on each floor and a stairway at the side. The lane becomes a walled path and gives widening views as it climbs above the village.

Continue upwards on the obvious path passing the remains of lead-mining and quarrying activities. Keep straight on up a wider grassy track, through a gate and past a small building on the right to reach another gate with a stile on either side.

Go through the stile on the right and follow the clear path ahead. Pass through a derelict wall and bear left to follow the wall on your left. Keep straight ahead, passing an underground reservoir on your right to eventually reach a rough lane. Go through the stile opposite and bear right to a step stile. Now keep to the wall on the left to go through a squeezer stile. Keep in the same direction down a clear path to emerge into another lane beside a wooden seat. 'Geoff', for whom the seat is a memorial, obviously enjoyed the panoramic view from here! Matlock town climbs the opposite hillside with the former Smedley's Hydro, now the County Council offices, in the centre. Another of John Smedley's creations, the Riber Castle 'folly', crowns the hill on the right.

Walk a few paces to your right and then turn left through a stile to continue down the hill towards Masson Lees Farm. Cross the farm track close to the farm and continue ahead through a stile beside a large tree. Keep straight on across two fields and past a group of large tree stumps. Just before the 'Limestone Way' continues through a stile beside a gate turn right along a grassy track. After the next stile turn left immediately to continue downhill with a wall on your left. The path is faint but go straight down, aiming for Greenhill Farm ahead. Bear right at the bottom of the slope to meet the wall below the farm then keep the wall on your left down a shallow valley. When you meet another clear grassy path turn right onto it and follow it around the contour and into the woods of Shining Cliff, beside a wall on the left. Through the trees can be seen glimpses of the sheer limestone cliff of High Tor on the opposite side of the gorge. From far below comes the sound of the unseen traffic and the occasional train, which share this narrow valley with the river.

Continue to a tarmac road where you turn right and pass the tiny Chapel of St John, high above a roadside well. It is a curious little church built in 1897. When you reach a gate across the road, immediately before Cliffe House, you have a choice of routes.

For a magnificent view across to High Tor, albeit on a slightly more strenuous route, turn right up the narrow path signposted to the Heights of Abraham. The path climbs beside a wall then continues across open ground and becomes walled again as it passes Masson Farm. Cross a stile close to the farm and continue ahead to a footpath sign. Following the signpost climb to a stile beside a gate then go along a clear grassy track which eventually brings you to an entry gate to the Heights of Abraham.

A little way above the gate go through a stile and follow the obvious path alongside the boundary fence, across a track and into the trees. Continue along this path until you finally emerge from the wood at the footpath sign near Ember Farm. Turn left and retrace your steps down through the trees to Matlock Bath.

However, for an easier return from Cliffe House to Matlock Bath follow the signposted footpath on the left. This winds through the woods, passing beneath the cable cars and finally descending to the road you climbed at the start of the walk. Turn left to return to the car.

Walk 15:
Milldale and Alstonefield

As well as a pleasant stretch beside the River Dove this walk gives superb views from above the dale and passes through the attractive village of Alstonefield.

Despite several short steep climbs this is not an over-strenuous walk. However, after prolonged rain it can be very muddy in places and the first stretch close to the river may be particularly difficult. In wet weather, especially in winter, wellies or walking boots are essential.

Distance: *5.5 miles (9km).*

Parking: *Public car park at Milldale.*
Map reference 137548.

Many of the lanes and footpaths of this walk were established packhorse routes in the Middle Ages, when Alstonefield had a thriving market. In spring masses of snowdrops and, later, daffodils line the lanes. The river itself is home to various water birds such as dippers, herons and wagtails. The River Dove has provided pleasure for walkers and anglers for centuries and its delights were recorded as early as 1653 by Izaak Walton in "The Compleat Angler".

Turn left out of the car park and follow the road to the village. Just before the bridge turn right up a steep footpath immediately after Old Millers Cottage. After a short climb cross a stile and follow the path along the hillside with the river below. The clear path takes you through a small wood and over several stiles before dropping to the river bank.

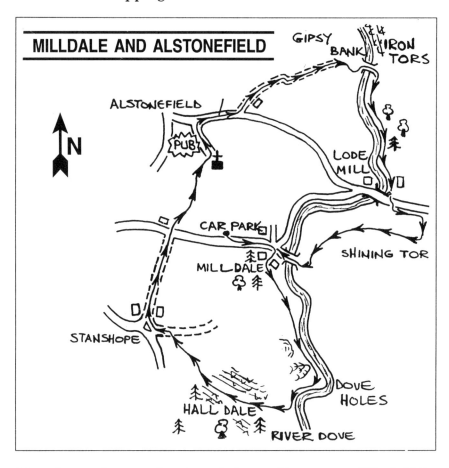

Now keep close to the river, below a limestone cliff. A little further along you get a good view of Dove Holes caves on the opposite bank. Eventually you reach a wide grassy area, just before a wall, at the foot of Hall Dale. Turn right up Hall Dale, with the wall close on your left. The path is steep at first but soon becomes more gradual. Keep straight ahead following the stiles across the fields when you come to the top of the dale. In the final large field, as you aim towards the farm ahead you get gradually closer to the wall on your left. Cross a stile over the wall then continue to another stile onto a rough lane.

Dove Holes Caves

Turn left and at the end of the lane turn right into a farm lane. Pass the fine old Stanshope Hall on your left, then a farm on your right and continue along a walled track. This eventually descends to a minor road at Dale Bottom. Go through a stile opposite and climb an obvious path up the hillside. Keep close to a hedge, later a wall, on your left and cross a stile beside a gate at the top.

Pass a large tree then keep the same direction over a large field, aiming to the left of the church ahead. Cross a stile about halfway along the wall at the top of the field. Continue forward beside a fence on your right to cross a stile over the fence, when you reach it. Now keep straight ahead to a walled path which brings you into the lane near Alstonefield church. The present church is mainly 16th century, although it replaced much earlier structures. Inside, the 17th century box pews remain, including the ornate family pew of the Cottons of nearby Beresford Hall. Charles Cotton was a friend of Izaak Walton and wrote a later addition to "The Compleat Angler" describing a journey through this part of Derbyshire.

Turn left and follow the lane to the centre of the village. Bear right past the George Inn to reach a road signposted to Lode Mill and Ashbourne. Turn right into it, past the former Wesleyan chapel and continue to the second footpath sign. Here turn left and follow the walled track known as Gipsy Lane, which 300 years ago was an established route to Bakewell. It eventually descends to a stile and a wonderful view of the River Dove and Iron Tors.

This is Gipsy Banks – reputedly a favoured meeting place in the past for Gipsies. Directly below is Coldeaton Bridge (formerly the site of a ford) but the way down may not be clear. Bear right down a shallow gulley, keeping straight on when it widens out. You eventually pick up the zig-zags of the old packhorse route and descend more gradually to the river. Cross the footbridge and turn right to follow the riverside path to the road at Lode Mill.

A few steps to the left on the opposite side of the road go through a small gate and turn left on a signposted footpath to Milldale via Shining Tor. (The shorter but very strenuous route to the right is not advisable!). The path climbs beside the road at first, then turns right on reaching a signpost to Milldale. Continue up Pinch Bank to the top of Shining Tor where you will find that your efforts are well rewarded by the stunning view!

The path along the top of the dale is quite clear. After eventually crossing a stile over the wall on your left, just above Milldale, you zig-zag down the hillside to the river once more to cross Viator's Bridge into Milldale. This packhorse bridge got its name from the Viator (traveller) in Charles Cotton's book who was amazed at its narrowness and the steepness of its approach.

Walk 16:
Monsal Dale and Litton Mill

A stroll through one of Derbyshire's most well-known valleys then a climb to the hills above, giving dramatic views.

Apart from a steep climb above Litton Mill the route is generally easy on clear tracks and field paths.

Distance: *About 5.5 miles (9km).*

Parking: *The public car park at Monsal Head. Map reference 185715.*

Go through the lower of the two stiles in the wall at the top of the road which descends from Monsal Head into the dale. Follow the steep path to the valley bottom then turn left around the end of the farm buildings and cross a footbridge over the River Wye.

At the far side bear right over a stile and climb the clear path, signposted to Brushfield and Taddington Dale. Immediately after crossing a bridge over the Monsal Trail climb another stile on the right then follow the path across two fields to reach a rough lane. Turn right down it and just before it goes underneath a bridge bear right through an access point onto the Monsal Trail.

This was the former Bakewell-Buxton branch of the LMR. Its construction was considered by early 'conservationists' to have destroyed the beauty and peace of the dale. Now the trains have gone and long stretches of the line have become public path-

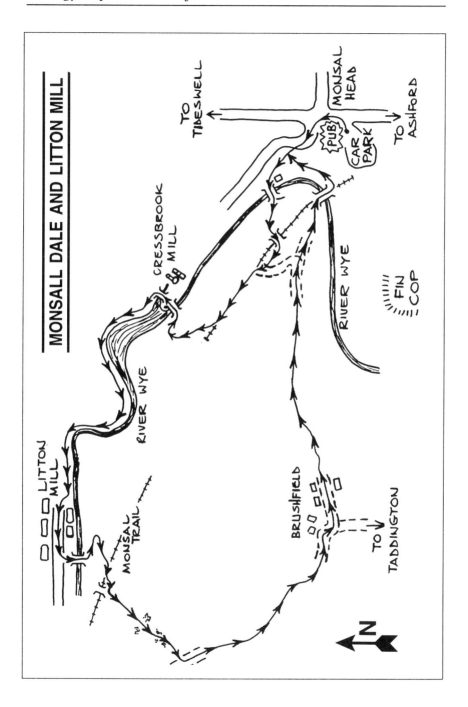

ways. On the small building just to the right is an interesting photograph of how this part of the railway looked many years ago. Turn left and walk along the Trail until you approach the blocked-up entrance to Cressbrook Tunnel where you go through a gate on your right. Follow the clear path along the hillside, gradually descending past Cressbrook Mill and eventually turning sharp right down some rocky steps to cross a footbridge just below a weir.

Cressbrook was a cotton-spinning mill, originally one of Richard Arkwright's. Looking towards the mill you see above the trees the building which housed the child apprentices, with a strange Gothic folly at the end of it. In the early 19th century many mills employed child labourers, often from the workhouses of large cities. Those at Cressbrook were well treated compared to apprentices working in many mills, who were often subjected to harsh and brutal regimes.

The Apprentice House, Cressbrook Mill

The wide stretch of river, dammed to provide water power for the mill, is now home to a wide variety of water birds. Go forward and bear left over a small bridge and continue beside the river, beneath a limestone cliff. Follow the riverside path through the delightfully named Water-cum-Jolly Dale to eventually reach Litton Mill. The route turns right to cross the millstream and then left to pass between the mill buildings, on a surfaced road. Litton Mill was also a cotton-spinning mill. The recollections of one of the apprentices of the brutalities he suffered here was used later in his life to help improve the dreadful conditions in factories.

Shortly after leaving the mill turn through a wall on your left to continue along a narrow path signposted to the Monsal Trail and Taddington. Cross the millstream and the river and climb through the trees to emerge onto the Trail again. Turn right and immediately before a bridge over the Trail climb the steps on your left. At the top cross a stile on your left and bear slightly right to climb steeply up the hillside. The path is clear at first and when it becomes less distinct the route is shown by several marker posts among the bushes. As you climb, an extensive view unfolds, The pattern of limestone walls near Tideswell is particularly impressive.

Cross the remains of a wall and continue uphill through old lead workings, with a wall now on your right. When you come to a stile over the wall cross it and continue upwards, bearing slightly right, to the top of the hill. Go through further lead workings to walk with a wall on your left, crossing a stile over this wall when you reach it. Now there is a wide view forwards to Taddington. Go straight ahead beside the wall on your left to cross a stile into a walled lane.

Turn left to follow the lane through several gates and past a group of farm buildings on the right. Continue through trees to pass Middle Farm buildings on the left. Where the lane bends right towards Taddington turn left on the track signposted to Monsal Dale. Go through a gate then a farm to continue on the wide track above the wooded Taddington Dale. Go through another two gates and cross a stretch of open grassland to approach two gateways. Leave the track here and go straight ahead through the left-hand gateway on a footpath signposted to the Monsal Trail and Upperdale.

Cross two fields with the wall on your right then continue on a walled track above Monsal Dale. Across the valley is the steep hillside of Fin Cop with the imposing remains of an Iron Age fort on top. Continue ahead following the clear track as it starts to descend to Upperdale. Over the wall on your left was the Putwell Hill lead mine. The derelict chimney which can be seen from further down the track is one of the very few remaining on the site of a lead mine in Derbyshire, and was constructed for what was thought to be the only underground steam engine in the county.

Where the track bends sharply left keep straight ahead down an enclosed bridleway. At the bottom go through a gate to regain the Monsal Trail. Turn right and cross the viaduct to turn left just before the tunnel and climb the path through the trees back to Monsal Head.

Walk 17:
Monsal Dale, Cressbrook and Longstone Edge

The first half of this walk is through limestone dales, initially wooded but then with rough grassy slopes often rich in flowers. You return over wide fields and the heather-covered Longstone Edge from which there are magnificent views.

The walk has several long, gradual climbs and one very steep one.

Distance: Almost 8 miles (12.5km).

Parking: The public car park at Monsal Head. Map reference 185715.

Go through the lower of two stiles in the wall at the top of the road leading from Monsal Head down into the dale. Descend a steep path to the valley floor, ignoring a path to the left part way down. Turn left around the end of farm buildings and cross a footbridge over the river. Turn immediately right through a stile and climb the clear path to go over a bridge and through a stile. Continue ahead into a rough track and turn right down it to reach the Monsal Trail.

Turn left and follow the Trail until as you approach a blocked tunnel you turn right through a gate. A clear path descends gently towards Cressbrook Mill where it drops more steeply through trees and crosses a footbridge beside the weir. Bear

MONSAL DALE, CRESSBROOK AND LONGSTONE EDGE

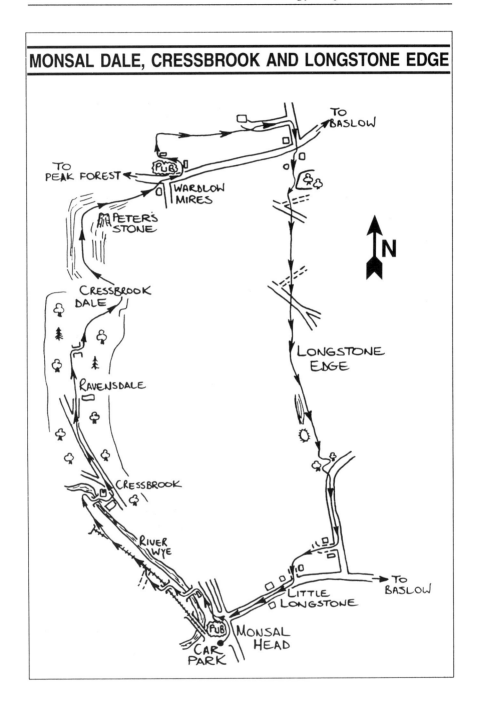

right through the mill yard and pass the derelict mill building to reach a surfaced road. Built originally by Richard Arkwright, Cressbrook Mill was later acquired by the poet William Newton, known as the 'Minstrel of the Peak', who had earlier worked as a carpenter there. He gained a reputation for treating his child apprentices with a consideration for their well-being not normally found in millowners of the time. His young workers were well fed and housed and attended church and Sunday school.

Cressbrook Mill

Turn left and keeping right at a fork climb steadily up a quiet tree-shaded road. Eventually turn right off it down a no-through-road to Ravensdale. The picturesque cottages you pass were once occupied by workers at Cressbrook Mill and bore the

curious name of Bury-Me-Wick. In the cliff above them, probably the home of the ravens which gave the dale its name, is a
cave which has yielded evidence of occupation during the Stone
Age. Beyond the cottages continue ahead beside a (usually) dry
stream bed, through trees then along the foot of a steep, grassy
slope.

Peter's Stone in Cressbrook Dale

Turn right over a footbridge and continue up an obvious path through Cressbrook Nature Reserve. Ignore a path to the left and climb steadily, leaving the trees and finally reaching a wonderful viewpoint above a bend in the dale, which makes the climb well worthwhile. In late spring the limestone slopes all around are carpeted with early purple orchids interspersed with cowslips, mountain pansies, wood anemones and water avens.

Bear left down a clear path and continue ahead along the bottom of the dale. After passing beneath a limestone outcrop known as Peter's Stone, the dale opens out and you finally go through a gate close to a house and reach a main road at Wardlow Mires. A turnpike toll-house stood beside this road junction and in 1815 the widow who kept the toll-gate was robbed and murdered. The murderer was caught, hanged and his body displayed on a gibbet nearby. A similar fate befell Black Harry, a notorious highwayman of the district, a hundred years previously.

Cross the main road and turn right. Just beyond the Three Stags Head pub turn left through a gate and bear left between farm buildings. Bear right at the end of the farmyard, as directed, to find a small gate between the side of a barn and the boundary wall. Go straight ahead over two fields, with a wall on your left, then bear right across the third to a stile in the top corner. Now keep straight on over several fields, with a wall on your left for much of the way. In the final field, as you approach a caravan site, with a farm to your left, bear slightly left to a small metal gate in the field corner. Turn right and follow the farm drive to a surfaced road.

Turn right and continue to a main road. Go straight across and climb a stile on your right at the start of the farm track. Follow a path to the left past a duckpond and continue ahead on a fairly clear path which soon bears right, making towards the right-hand end of some trees. Pass close to the trees on your left then bear right away from them, cross a farm driveway and continue across a field corner to a minor road.

Cross a stile almost opposite and bear left up a large field to a stile about half way along the wall at the top. Keep the same direction over two more fields, a narrow rough patch of land and a further field to cross a rough track and reach a minor road. Cross the road and follow the footpath towards Great Long-stone across two fields, then an area of old mine heaps to a stile by some wooden posts. Bear slightly left over more lead work-ings and follow a fairly clear path ahead which climbs gradually through heather to a footpath sign at the top of Longstone Edge. At one thousand feet above sea level, there are splendid all-round views from here.

Keep straight ahead, descending slightly then going over level ground which shows signs of more recent opencast work-ing. After going alongside a hollow on the right the path descends to a stile beside a gate. Follow the clear path steeply down through trees, bearing right to cross more restored work-ings and finally go down some wooden steps to a track and onto the road.

Walk down the road for some distance and then turn right onto a track at a sign for Dale Farm. Where the track turns right beyond the farm, continue ahead over a stile. Keep straight on until immediately beyond a house on your left you turn left over a stile into a grassy track which brings you onto the road at Little Longstone. Turn right and follow the road through the village, where you pass the stocks and the pinfold, and back to Monsal Head.

Walk 18:
Offerton Moor and Shatton

After crossing the River Derwent by stepping stones you climb to open moorland heights which give wide-ranging views over the Derwent and Hope Valleys.

An initial long, steep climb followed by easy walking on clear paths and lanes. NB. The stepping stones over the Derwent can be submerged after periods of heavy rain or snow.

Distance: About 5 miles (8.5km).

Parking: In a lay-by on the A625 to the west of Hathersage. Map reference 222817.

Map: The Ordnance Survey map most useful on this walk is: "Sheffield (Sheet SK 28/38)" from the Pathfinder series.

Walk a short distance along the road towards Hathersage and turn right through a stile beside a gate. Follow the path down to the river and continue with the river on your left to eventually cross the stepping stones. Dippers, the stumpy brown and white birds which walk under the water to search for food, are frequently spotted along here.

Now keep straight ahead, between two stone posts, to climb the hill with a line of bushes on your right. Bear slightly right after the second stile to go through a gate and into a surfaced lane. Turn left to follow the lane, passing Offerton Hall on your left. This beautiful Tudor manor house is reputedly one of seven

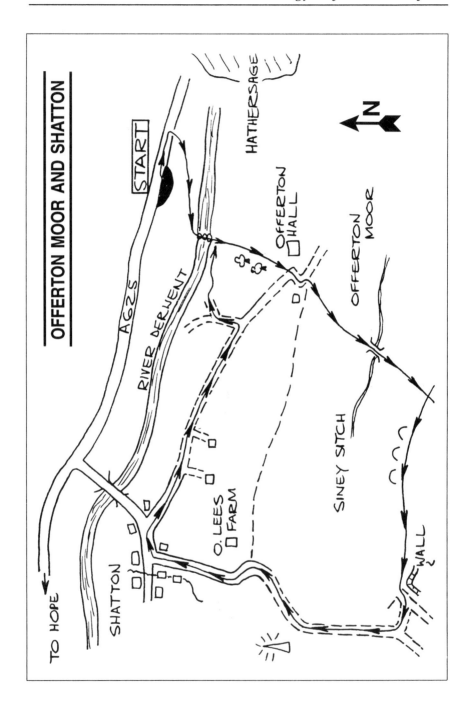

houses built by Robert Eyre of Hathersage for his seven sons, all within sight of each other. In more recent times it was a Youth Hostel.

Just after the entrance to the Hall, as the road levels out, are two stiles on the right. Climb the second one and go uphill on a clear path which soon curves right. When the path forks, just beyond a spring, keep right and climb steeply on a wide grassy track to the top of the hill. A magnificent view unfolds as you climb. Across the valley fields reach up to the rocks at Stanage Edge, with Higger Tor to the right and Win Hill to the left. Ladybower Dam is revealed and the Derwent Moors beyond. A summer migrant bird to be seen in this upland area is the ring ouzel, which resembles a blackbird with a white collar.

Keep to the obvious path over Offerton Moor, crossing a footbridge over the Siney Sitch. When you begin to descend, with Abney directly ahead, look out for another clear path crossing the one you are on and turn right onto it. The path is easily followed and soon you pass some shooting butts and follow a wall on your left. Eventually cross a stile over a fence by a wall corner and keep straight on with the fence on your right. Soon the wall returns close on the left and almost immediately turn right onto a rutted track. Follow the track and soon bear right between stone posts into a walled green lane.

Now follow this lane past a TV mast and down off the moor. Part way down the tall chimney of Hope cement works becomes visible. Although this is an ugly intrusion on a pastoral landscape it provides welcome employment for the Hope Valley. The road becomes surfaced and finally brings you into Shatton. This pleasant hamlet is of ancient foundation, recorded as 'Scetune' in the Domesday Book. Shatton Hall, another of the Eyre family houses, lies a little to the west of the hamlet and there are other equally old farmhouses.

Pass the end of Towngate Lane, with its ford, on your left and then bear right where the road forks. Follow this lane until it bends sharply right uphill. Here go straight ahead through a gate and continue along the wide track signposted to Offerton. After climbing briefly continue downhill to cross a stream. Soon, just beyond a gate on the left, turn left through two stone gateposts then immediately left again through a wire fence. Continue with the fence on your right, cross a stream and follow the clear track by the stream to the River Derwent. Now turn right onto a path which, after crossing a footbridge, continues beside the river to return to the stepping stones.

Retrace your steps back to the start.

Stepping stones over the River Derwent

Walk 19:
Taddington, Chelmorton and Flagg

A walk linking three peaceful villages of the limestone uplands and including an optional visit to an ancient burial site.

After a short, steep climb from Taddington the going is fairly gentle.

Distance: *5.5 miles (9km).*

Parking: *Roadside parking in Taddington.*
Map reference 143711.

Just above Taddington church, at the start of the road to Flagg, is a signposted footpath on the right. Follow this narrow path between the houses then bear right to climb two fields and reach a metalled road. Continue up the path opposite, signposted to Chelmorton. After passing a derelict wall corner on your right keep in the same direction across another derelict wall. Make towards the right of some bushes when they come into view ahead and cross a signposted stile at a wall corner. As you climb a really magnificent view is revealed, extending over many miles of the White Peak. Continue in the same direction, crossing a stile to the left of an underground reservoir and reaching a squeezer stile by the gate ahead.

Now, with the wall on your right for most of the way, follow the stiles across fields, a rough track and more fields to eventually reach a metalled road. Here you may wish to make a short diversion to see Five Wells Barrow. This is a neolithic burial mound containing two chambered tombs in which were found the remains of twelve burials. The mound itself is unusual being constructed of small pieces of quarried stone rather than stones from the surface of the ground. To reach it turn right and follow a rough track which leaves the lane at a bend. A little way along a concessionary footpath on the right leads to the site.

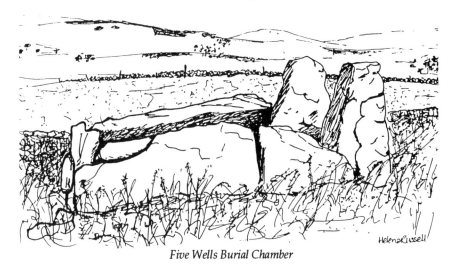

Five Wells Burial Chamber

Returning to the route of the walk go through a squeezer stile on the opposite side of the lane. Follow a clear path beside a deep lead rake. As you descend towards Chelmorton you get a good view of the church's most unusual weather-vane – a locust! (The church is dedicated to St John the Baptist, and the locust motif is repeated on the long kneeler at the altar rail.) Just before you reach the surfaced road above the church notice the stone water troughs on your right. The spring which feeds these used to be the water source for the village, running beside the village street, and bears the delightful name of the Illy-Willy Water.

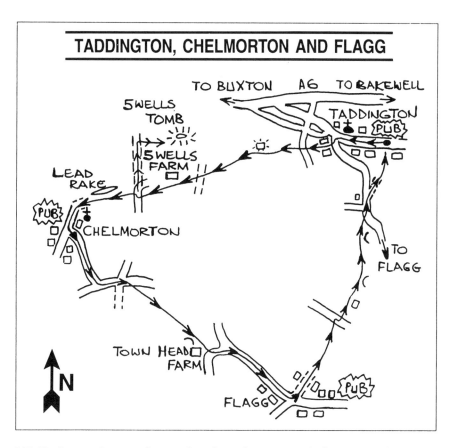

TADDINGTON, CHELMORTON AND FLAGG

Walk down the road past the church on your left. It is well worth a visit being very much in keeping with the peacefulness of the village and containing a 14th century stone chancel screen and several fine stone coffin lids. Just beyond the church turn left up Church Lane. As you climb gradually you can see the long narrow fields surrounding Chelmorton. These resulted from the enclosure of the ancient 'strip' field system into larger units. They date from long before the 17th and 18th century Enclosure Acts, possibly as early as AD 600 – 800.

On reaching a T-junction turn left and keep straight on at the next junction. Just beyond this turn right through a squeezer stile and bear left across the field, passing close to a wall corner on your right. Continue in the same direction, getting gradually closer to the wall on your left and cross the stile near a large tree on your left. Keep the same line, on a fairly clear path, and climb three more stiles, the third one beside a gateway. Now continue straight ahead passing spoil heaps and Town Head Farm on your right to emerge into a narrow lane. Turn left and then right at the road junction.

Continue through the small village of Flagg, noted for its annual point-to-point meeting. This very popular meeting is held on the Tuesday of Easter week and is run over the surrounding fields, with the field boundaries providing the jumps. Turn left up a tree-lined driveway, almost opposite the telephone box and the former school building. Pass a large well-built barn with a 17th century datestone and go straight across the farmyard and through a gate into a field. Keep straight ahead, at first with a wire fence on your right, then go through a gateway and across a large field to reach a surfaced road.

Turn right and soon left over another stile, walk up a long narrow field past a farm on your right and eventually go through a stile in the wall on your right. Bear left to another stile, then keep the same direction to the left of a grassy mound and go through a gateway in the field corner. Continue on the faint path through another gateway and keep the same line up the next field to a step stile at the top. Continue in the same direction over two more stiles then bear slightly right around a hump of ground and go through a gateway. The final stile is near the top right-hand corner of the next field and brings you onto a minor road.

Continue ahead on the Taddington road, passing a barn on your left, and turn off right down a rough, walled lane. This becomes a narrow footpath which brings you back to the main street of Taddington.

Walk 20:
The Upper Dove Valley

Dovedale must be one of the Peak District's most popular attractions. Yet above Hartington the River Dove flows through a wider, equally attractive though much quieter valley. This walk takes you along and above the valley, giving superb views.

A generally easy walk with one short, steep climb.

Distance: 7 miles (11km).

Parking: In Hartington.
Map reference 128604.

A picturesque and much-visited village, Hartington lies close to the River Dove, which forms the boundary between Derbyshire and Staffordshire. Clustered around a market place (a Market Charter was granted in 1203) and a pond its many fine buildings include a classical style market hall and the 17th century Hartington Hall (now a Youth Hostel). St Giles' church is mainly 14th century and contains some interesting carving, an octagonal font and an effigy of a woman who appears to be tucked under a blanket!

Leave the village by the road which passes the church and climb steadily to reach a footpath sign to Pilsbury on your left, immediately after a farm and barn. Follow the signpost over three fields and in the fourth bear left to a gateway onto a farm track. A little way down the track, where it bends sharp left, go straight ahead through a gateway.

Keep near a wall on your right at first and when it turns right bear very slightly left then go straight forward, passing the ends of two short stretches of wall on your left. Continue ahead over ground strewn with limestone rocks, bearing slightly right to cross a stile where two dilapidated walls meet. Keep straight on over the next field, cross a stile and go through old lead workings to reach another stile. Lead mining was formerly an important industry throughout the limestone areas of Derbyshire. The humps and hollows of disturbed ground, such as you see around you now, are frequent indicators of mining activity, being the heaps of waste material left after the lead ore was

The former Hartington Market Hall

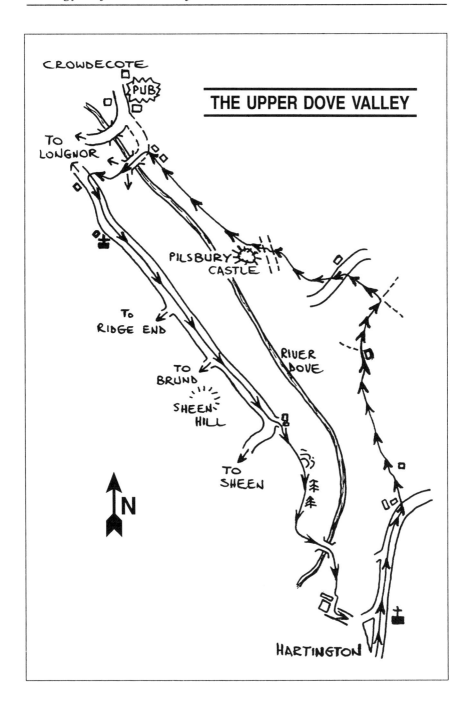

extracted. Keep on ahead, climbing slightly, on a faint path. Just before a gateway bear slightly right to reach a stile made of large stones. Now follow a clear path towards a ruined farm among some trees. Go through a gateway and pass close to the farm on your right to reach a gate just beyond it.

From the gate bear right passing close to a few trees on your right and climb to a wall above a rocky outcrop. Follow the wall ahead and where it turns right bear right to pass another wall corner on your right. Continue in the same direction, cross a rough track and then climb a step stile over the next wall. Walk beside a wall on your right to the valley floor. Turn left along the path to Pilsbury and reach a surfaced road close to a barn.

Walk a few yards to your left along the road then cross a stile through the wall on your right, signposted to Crowdecote and Longnor. Cross the first field in the direction shown and then go straight ahead with a wall on your right through two more stiles. Pilsbury Castle is now in view below and the path soon descends to it. Pilsbury Castle was a fortification of the motte and bailey type, built probably not long after the Norman invasion of England. The siting of a castle here shows the importance of controlling the upper reaches of the Dove in those times.

Near a gate cross a stile through the boundary wall of the castle site and turn right to follow the obvious path around the base of a rocky pinnacle and down to a stile beside a gateway. Now follow the path across the fields with the river to your left and the unmistakable 'point' of Parkhouse Hill ahead. The path eventually becomes a wider track, enclosed at first, which brings you to a farm on your right. Just past the farm go through a stile into a walled lane. The route, signposted to Sheen and Longnor, turns left here to a footbridge over the Dove. However, if you wish to explore the hamlet of Crowdecote continue ahead on the walled lane. The appropriately named Packhorse

Inn and an old toll cottage show the former importance of Crowdecote's position above an ancient crossing of the Dove.

Cross the **footbridge** over the river and continue forward on the footpath to Edgetop. Climb straight up the hill with bushes on your right and cross a stile through a wall near the top of the field. Now go forward between bushes and after crossing a dry ditch bear slightly right and climb towards a wall at the top of the slope. The path becomes fairly clear and reaches a stile through the wall near a footpath sign.

Knowsley Farm

From the road here there is a wonderful view back down to Crowdecote and over the hills around the head of the Dove, with Axe Edge in the distance. Turn left and walk along the quiet road. Soon you go uphill, passing Knowsley Farm with its dovecote. Just beyond is Knowsley Cross, the shaft of an ancient marker cross set on a restored base in 1899. Now continue on the level, with the valley of the Dove to the left and the much gentler Manifold valley to the right. Keep straight on, passing two road junctions on the right and the strangely shaped Sheen Hill. When you come to a farm on the left, at a point where the road bends right, go through a stile beside the gate and into the farmyard. Bear right alongside the wall to find a narrow path between the end of a farm building and the wall and reach a field.

Now follow the stiles ahead to reach a fir plantation. Keep to the path along the top edge of the plantation and continue with the wall on your right to eventually turn left down a deeply hollowed path. Where the path becomes unclear go forward through some bushes to find a stile across a wire fence onto a track. Cross the track and keep straight on to a footbridge over the river. Beyond the bridge bear right and follow the clear path towards Hartington. As you approach the left-hand side of the cheese factory, which still produces the popular Hartington Stilton, cross a stile through the hedge on your left. Turn right to walk alongside the factory to the road. Turn left along the road to the village centre.

Walk 21:
White Edge

A bracing walk, with fine views, along the gritstone edges above the Derwent Valley.

After a short climb onto White Edge the route is level and easily followed.

Distance: *Just over 5 miles (8.5km).*

Parking: *The walk description starts from the public car park at Curbar Gap (map reference 263748) but alternatively you can start from Hay Wood public car park (map reference, 256778).*

Cross the stile beside a gate alongside the entrance to the car park. Over the stile, a little to the right, is a tall guide stone. Several packhorse routes met at Curbar Gap and this stone shows the way to 'Shefield', Dronfield, 'Chesterfeild' and 'Tidswall' (Tideswell). (For more on guide stones see the Chatsworth and Ball Cross walk.)

Go forward on the clear track with a wall to your left and at the wall corner keep straight ahead on the marked footpath. On reaching a second wall corner continue forward following the wall to cross a small stream and climb to the top of the fields. Turn left and follow the path, signposted to Longshaw, up onto White Edge.

After walking along the Edge for over a mile start looking to the right for another guide stone. This one's situation amongst

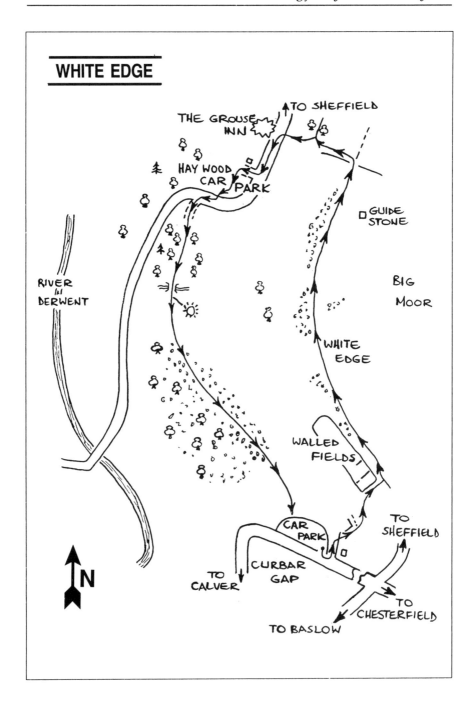

the heather and well away from present roads gives a clear indication of the importance of these waymarkers to travellers of former times. The stone has clear markings, showing the way to Dronfield and other nearby towns, and is well worth looking at.

On Curbar Edge

Soon, you go through a gap in a high wall and turn immediately left to follow the path towards the Grouse Inn. Keep beside the wall on your left at first, then bear right to the edge of a birch wood. Turn left and follow a bridleway through the wood. Go through a gate and cross a field to reach the road near the Grouse Inn.

Turn left and go along the road a little way before turning right down a rough track to Hay Wood car park. Turn left and walk through the car park, cross a stile on your right and follow the path over a stream and up to rejoin the road. Turn right and go along the road for a few paces before going through a gate on your left into the Eastern Moors Estate.

Follow the wide track through a scrubby birch wood. After crossing a stream near the end of the wood look for the remains of a stone circle on your left – a clear path leads to it from the main track. The earth banks and remaining stones suggest a double circle with an entrance marked by one much larger stone.

Continue on the clear track all the way along Froggatt and Curbar Edges until you return to the car park.

Walk 22: Win Hill

Following routes used by centuries of travellers coming over the surrounding hills, this walk climbs gently from a pleasant and interesting village to what must be one of the most spectacular viewpoints in the Peak District.

Although the outward climb is gradual, the return descent is very steep.

Distance: *Almost 7 miles (11km).*

Parking: *In Hope village.*
Map reference 172835.

Hope was a Saxon settlement and there is a Saxon preaching cross in the churchyard. There has been a Christian church here since at least 600AD. Eccles House and Eccles Place in the village take their names from the ancient British word for 'church' and indicate an age-old holy place. For centuries Hope has been an important market town and still holds a weekly agricultural market. It also holds a 'Wakes' festival and well-dressing every June and renowned sheep-dog trials later in the year.

Cross the road from the car park and go a little way to the right to turn left beside Blacksmith's Cottage on a footpath signposted to Losehill Farm. Shortly afterwards you pass a green, cast-iron sign, one of many erected by the Peak District and Northern Counties Footpath Society. Each one shows the

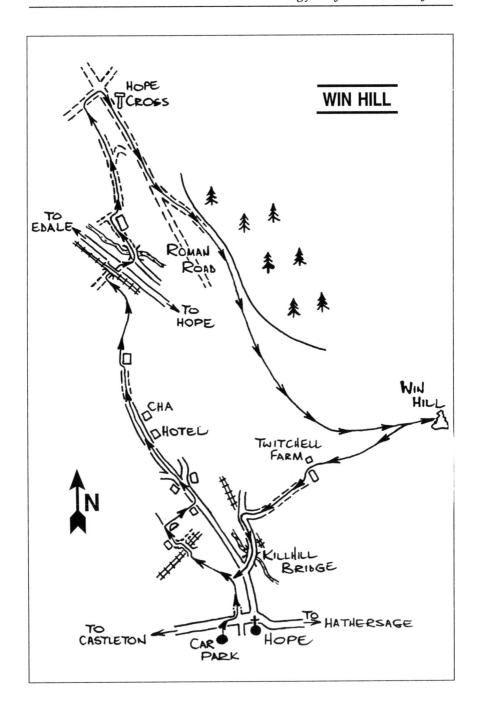

date of its erection. Founded in 1894 as the result of a long-running dispute over an ancient right of way across grouse moors the Peak District and Northern Counties Footpath Society was one of the earliest of countryside pressure groups. It is still active.

Continue straight ahead between modern houses then cross a road to go through a small gate beside a school on the right. Keep straight on over several fields, following the stiles and a clear path to reach a railway line. Cross the footbridge over the line. Turn left, into a lane, then right, as directed, to pass alongside a house. Just before reaching a stile and a footpath sign turn right beside an arched outbuilding to cross a stile into a field. Go straight ahead to reach the Hope to Edale road.

Turn left and a little way along the road bear left up a narrow, surfaced lane. Continue straight ahead, keeping right at a fork, to pass a hotel and then a CHA Guest House. To your left Lose Hill rises to its pointed summit while across the valley is the long ridge of Hope Brink. The lane becomes a track then at Oaker Farm it becomes a path, skirting the farm and continuing into fields beyond. In late June and early July the last large field presents a wonderful variety of flowers typical of an old hay meadow – yellow rattle, ox-eye daisies, clover and common spotted orchids. Eventually you climb a ladder stile and turn right down a track which goes under the railway and onto the road.

A few paces to the right go through the gate opposite and descend to the River Noe. Join the surfaced track and cross the bridge. Follow the track up to Edale End Farm, where a large barn has won a CPRE award for its renovation as a National Trust wardens' workshop, which includes an information shelter. Turn right around the end of the line of buildings then left through a gate to follow the clear track ahead. Climb a stile by another gate and continue straight ahead, on the wide track in the direction of Jaggers Clough.

At a fork, where the main track begins to go uphill, keep straight on along a grassy, level track which climbs gently to a stile at a gap in a wall. Beyond this the track becomes hollowed and climbs more steeply to reach a wide, rutted track. Turn right here and follow it to a footpath sign at a crossroads of tracks on top of the ridge.

Hope Cross

Turn right, following the direction to Win Hill and Hope, and walk along the former Roman road, which soon goes through a gate. The road linked the Roman fort at Navio, near Brough, with another fort, Melandra, near Glossop. Beyond the gate is Hope Cross, originally a mediaeval way-marker which bears the date of its restoration – 1737. It stands at a crossroads of ancient packhorse routes and shows the directions of Glossop, Hope, Edale and Sheffield (note the spelling of the last!).

Keep straight on, with a wonderful view of the Edale valley to the right. Immediately beyond another gate bear left off the Roman road up a clear track.

Up ahead across the valley the cement works and its towering chimney mar an otherwise idyllic scene. The works were in operation before 1951, when the National Park was created, and provide an important source of employment for local people. The Peak Park planners have to try and strike the difficult balance between protecting the countryside and protecting local communities by providing jobs. Although it provides many jobs it is very unlikely that the cement works would be sanctioned today as it intrudes significantly upon the Hope valley. However, the glorious views in many directions, some probably unsurpassed anywhere in Derbyshire, still make the climb very worthwhile.

Follow the obvious track along the ridge, initially alongside a plantation then over open ground, making towards the rocky prominence of Win Hill, and enjoying the panoramic views. According to legend the name of Win Hill dates from the time of a battle between the respective kings of Northumbria and Wessex. The victor camped on what became known as 'Win' Hill, the loser on the adjacent 'Lose' Hill.

After a final scramble to the summit and a rest to take in the magnificent view down to Ladybower Reservoir and the Ashopton Viaduct, retrace your steps a short way to where a wide path bears off left through the heather. Descend steadily to a stile into a field.

Go straight down and through a metal gate beside a footpath sign. Continue down through Twitchell Farm – the name Twitchell very appropriately means 'steep path'. Follow the farm driveway downhill and over a cattle grid, beyond which it bends right and joins a lane. Turn left and go under the railway. A little further on, you pass a more recent Peak District and Northern Counties Footpath Society sign on your left.

Continue ahead to cross Killhill Bridge (where the Roman road, having descended Hope Brink, crossed the River Noe) and reach the Edale road. Go over the stile opposite and follow a path which soon joins the one you started out on at the edge of a field. Turn left and retrace your steps to Hope village.

We publish guides to individual towns, plus books on walking and cycling in the great out-
doors throughout England and Wales. This is a recent selection:

Country Walking

LAKELAND WALKING: On The Level – Norman Buckley *(£6.95)*

FIFTY CLASSIC WALKS IN THE PENNINES – Terry Marsh *(£8.95)*

HILL WALKS IN MID WALES – Dave Ing *(£8.95)*

WEST PENNINE WALKS – Mike Cresswell *(£5.95)*

WELSH WALKS: Dolgellau /Cambrian Coast – L. Main & M. Perrott *(£5.95)*

WELSH WALKS: Aberystwyth & District – L. Main & M. Perrott *(£5.95)*

WALKS IN MYSTERIOUS WALES – Laurence Main *(£7.95)*

RAMBLES IN NORTH WALES – Roger Redfern *(£6.95)*

RAMBLES AROUND MANCHESTER – Mike Cresswell *(£5.95)*

EAST CHESHIRE WALKS – Graham Beech *(£5.95)*

CHALLENGING WALKS: NW England & N Wales – Ron Astley *(£7.95)*

LONDON BUS-TOP TOURIST – John Wittich *(£6.95)*

TEA SHOP WALKS IN THE CHILTERNS – Jean Patefield *(£6.95)*

BY-WAY TRAVELS SOUTH OF LONDON – Geoff Marshall *(£6.95)*

BY-WAY BIKING IN THE CHILTERNS – Henry Tindell *(£7.95)*

PUB WALKS IN SNOWDONIA – Laurence Main *(£6.95)*

BEST PUB WALKS AROUND CHESTER & THE DEE VALLEY – John Haywood *(£6.95)*

BEST PUB WALKS IN GWENT – Les Lumsdon *(£6.95)*

PUB WALKS IN POWYS – Les Lumsdon & Chris Rushton *(£6.95)*

BEST PUB WALKS IN PEMBROKESHIRE – Laurence Main *(£6.95)*

BEST PUB WALKS AROUND CENTRAL LONDON – Ruth Herman *(£6.95)*

BEST PUB WALKS IN ESSEX – Derek Keeble *(£6.95)*

More Pub Walks . . .

There are many more titles in our fabulous series of 'Pub Walks' books for just about
every popular walking area in the UK, all featuring access by public transport. We
label our more recent ones as 'best' to differentiate them from inferior competit

Explore the Lake District:

THE LAKELAND SUMMITS – Tim Synge *(£7.95)*
100 LAKE DISTRICT HILL WALKS – Gordon Brown *(£7.95)*
LAKELAND ROCKY RAMBLES: Geology beneath your feet – Brian Lynas *(£7.95)*
FULL DAYS ON THE FELLS: Challenging Walks – Adrian Dixon *(£7.95)*
PUB WALKS IN THE LAKE DISTRICT – Neil Coates *(£6.95)*
LAKELAND WALKING, ON THE LEVEL – Norman Buckley *(£6.95)*
MOSTLY DOWNHILL: LEISURELY WALKS, LAKE DISTRICT – Alan Pears *(£6.95)*

Cycling . . .

CYCLE UK! The essential guide to leisure cycling – Les Lumsdon *(£9.95)*
OFF-BEAT CYCLING IN THE PEAK DISTRICT – Clive Smith *(£6.95)*
MORE OFF-BEAT CYCLING IN THE PEAK DISTRICT – Clive Smith *(£6.95)*
50 BEST CYCLE RIDES IN CHESHIRE – edited by Graham Beech *(£7.95)*
CYCLING IN THE COTSWOLDS – Stephen Hill *(£6.95)*
CYCLING IN THE CHILTERNS – Henry Tindell *(£7.95)*
CYCLING IN THE LAKE DISTRICT – John Wood *(£7.95)*
CYCLING IN LINCOLNSHIRE – Penny & Bill Howe *(£7.95)*
CYCLING IN NOTTINGHAMSHIRE – Penny & Bill Howe *(£7.95)*
CYCLING IN STAFFORDSHIRE – Linda Wain *(£7.95)*
CYCLING IN THE WEST COUNTRY – Helen Stephenson *(£7.95)*
CYCLING IN SOUTH WALES – Rosemary Evans *(£7.95)*
CYCLING IN NORTH WALES – Philip Routledge *(£7.95) ... available 1996*

Sport . . .

RED FEVER: from Rochdale to Rio as 'United' supporters – Steve Donoghue *(£7.95)*
UNITED WE STOOD: unofficial history of the Ferguson years – Richard Kurt *(£6.95)*
MANCHESTER CITY: Moments to Remember – John Creighton *(£9.95)*

- plus many more entertaining and educational books being regularly added to our list.
All of our books are available from your local bookshop. In case of difficulty, or to obtain our
complete catalogue, please contact:

eisure, 1 South Oak Lane, Wilmslow, Cheshire SK9 6AR
⁀ₐ: 01625 – 531035   Fax: 01625 – 536800

/ders welcome – call our friendly sales staff or use our 24 hour Answer-
st orders are despatched on the day we receive your order – you could
ɔur books in just a couple of days. Please add £2 p&p to all orders.